Praise for *What to Do Next*

My good friend Jeff Henderson has done it again! What a timely resource for so many people who are considering *what to do next*. Jeff walked this road personally and has chosen to use what he has learned to help others along the journey. What a beautiful picture of servant leadership! The road to what's next will certainly be challenging, but always remember that everything worthwhile is uphill. I wouldn't be endorsing this book if I didn't believe these pages will help you take the next step. So I join Jeff by echoing these words of encouragement: Just. Keep. Walking.

Dr. John C. Maxwell, Maxwell Leadership founder

The Great Resignation has resulted in millions of people wondering what's next for them. It's one of the reasons I'm excited about Jeff Henderson's book. His practical and winsome approach will have you highlighting, laughing, and enjoying the story. All the while, he'll help you take important steps toward figuring out what's next for you.

Michael Hyatt, *New York Times* bestselling author

If you're trying to figure out what to do next, Jeff Henderson thoughtfully guides you to make meaningful decisions in the midst of uncertainty. In this thought-provoking and practical read, you'll gain the confidence to identify your next steps—even if your next steps don't feel so obvious right now.

Valorie Burton, CEO of the Coaching and Positive Psychology Institute

As a fellow restless traveler who took a career leap of faith in my fifties, I found comfort in Jeff Henderson's journey. Whether you're contemplating a life change or just seeking validation for the direction you've taken, take a deep breath and read Jeff's book. I'm grateful he shared my story as an example of how to find your calling and follow it. Change is hard. But Jeff Henderson helps make it easier.

STEPHANIE STUCKEY, CEO, Stuckey's

In an era when millions of people are facing a seemingly infinite set of career options and rethinking their futures, Jeff Henderson arrives with a thoughtful, highly practical, and generous book. If you're looking for actionable strategies and wise counsel, pull up a chair and let Jeff coach you.

CAREY NIEUWHOF, bestselling author of At Your Best
and founder of The Art of Leadership Academy

Reading this book is like having a million-dollar coach in your corner helping you navigate your next move confidently.

SANGRAM VAJRE, cofounder of Terminus and Wall
Street Journal bestselling author of MOVE

Authentic. Helpful. Freeing. If all of our invitations to take a step of faith made sense and were easy, I doubt we would ever be super dependent on God. I love how this book empowers readers to not let the overwhelming nature of fear about the future keep them from the immediacy of obedience today. What to Do Next is a must-read resource for anyone looking for clarity, empowerment, and vision for what's ahead.

SHELLEY GIGLIO, cofounder of Passion
Conferences and Passion City Church

What you are about to read is a powerful reminder that what's next is worth it. Jeff Henderson has a unique way of capturing things crisply and openly and letting us into his world—a world full of wisdom and heart, honesty and insights. There is no one I trust and respect more than Jeff. I'm so glad he took the time to pen this timely book. What a gift, just like the guy who wrote it.

GLEN JACKSON, cofounder of Jackson Spalding marketing agency

My raving endorsement of Jeff Henderson's book may be biased. It came to me at precisely the moment I needed it. So to maintain integrity, I can only recommend *What to Do Next* to the person who wants to leave well, gain radical self-awareness, deepen wisdom, and feel incredibly confident in the direction they choose to go next. If you're not looking for any of that, don't bother reading this.

JOSEPH KING BARKLEY, speaker, executive
coach, and author of *Will > Want*

What to Do Next is a compelling guide to making the next right decision for your future. Jeff Henderson lays out helpful principles and thought-provoking insights that will help any professional make a good transition well their next season. I wish I'd had this book when I was making my last big professional transition!

GERALD FADAYOMI, author and lead pastor, Home Church Roswell

We all face pivotal moments that change everything and leave us feeling scared, stuck, and, most of all, wondering what to do next. In the last two years, millions of people have been feeling exactly that. That's why Jeff Henderson's book is coming at the perfect time. He gives you the steps you're looking for to be able to move forward and the encouragement you need to take them.

CHRISTY WRIGHT, #1 national bestselling author and speaker

Jeff Henderson is one of the most trusted voices in my life. His wisdom and honesty, which are on display in *What to Do Next*, guide you not only to the next right decision, but also give permission to hope and grieve and trust and try. This is the guidebook for what's next.

ANNIE F. DOWNS, *New York Times* bestselling author of *That Sounds Fun*

The reason *What to Do Next* is such a life-changing book is that the author hasn't simply researched the topic of career change; he has successfully navigated it multiple times. Jeff Henderson has written a personal and practical guide for everyone who cares about their future. If you don't think you need to read this book, just open it up. You will change your mind. *What to Do Next* will be one of those timeless classics you keep as reference for the next time you wonder, *Is it time to take a leap?*

REGGIE JOINER, founder and CEO of Orange

WHAT TO DO NEXT

WHAT TO DO
NEXT

Taking Your Best Step When Life Is Uncertain

JEFF HENDERSON

Author of *Know What You're FOR*

ZONDERVAN
BOOKS

ZONDERVAN BOOKS

What to Do Next
Copyright © 2022 by The FOR Company, LLC

Requests for information should be addressed to:
Zondervan, 3900 Sparks Dr. SE, Grand Rapids, Michigan 49546

Zondervan titles may be purchased in bulk for educational, business, fundraising, or sales promotional use. For information, please email SpecialMarkets@Zondervan.com.

ISBN 978-0-310-36607-2 (hardcover)
ISBN 978-0-310-36609-6 (audio)
ISBN 978-0-310-36608-9 (ebook)

Published in association with Yates & Yates, www.yates2.com.

Cover design: Alyssa Kang
Interior design: Denise Froehlich

Printed in the United States of America

22 23 24 25 26 27 28 29 30 /LSC/ 13 12 11 10 9 8 7 6 5 4 3 2 1

To Jesse and Cole,
always and forever,
no matter what.

Perhaps this is the moment
you were created for.

ESTHER 4:14 (PARAPHRASE)

Contents

I was walking to the finish line. Emotionally, I was limping to it.

It was the final day of September 2020, and my last day as lead pastor of Gwinnett Church in Atlanta, Georgia. I was making a career change in the middle of a global pandemic.

Who does that? I thought to myself. I would soon discover I wasn't alone.

The team surprised me with an outdoor farewell. Suddenly there I was, holding hands with my wife, Wendy, and daughter, Jesse, as we were walking down a path toward our car to drive away—to where, I wasn't quite sure.

Friends and coworkers, minutes away from being former coworkers, were on both sides waving, clapping, smiling. They had created an actual finish line that we were walking toward. After two previous days of rain, the sky was very bright, very blue.

We walked slowly. *Take it all in*, I reminded myself. I

knew this was the final moment of certainty I would have for quite a while.

I've visited the land of uncertainty before. Finishing one season while moving toward the next—it's one wild ride.

Your last day on the job is an odd combination of a graduation and a divorce. Depending on your situation, one may weigh heavier than the other. Still, your life is about to go through a massive change. There's an upheaval in your rhythms. Relationships inevitably change. Your identity takes a hit, and you wonder if your best days are behind you.

Or maybe that's just me. I walked slower, but the thoughts came faster.

What are you doing?

Is this a mistake?

Is it too late to call it off?

What if this is as good as it gets?

I'm so grateful.

I'm going to miss this place, these people.

Who has the keys to my car?

I gotta figure out what to do next.

Random, fast, emotions-to-the-brim thoughts.

I'm on the other side of that walk now. If Elon Musk would hurry up and figure out time travel, there's so much

I would like to go back and tell myself on that last day in September.

Hey, don't freak out, but it's me from the future. Yes, Elon figured it out. More importantly, just keep walking. It's going to be hard, but it's going to be worth it. Let's be honest. You don't really know what's next. Just. Keep. Walking. You can find what's next if you keep walking.

That's a good word from Future Me, but still, leaving your job and walking away toward uncertainty and not knowing what's next is harder than it looks.

In my case, I was walking away from a nonprofit I helped launch. Two of them actually. I was walking away from people I hired. Not just coworkers, but in my mind, family.

I named this nonprofit, helped raise the money for three buildings to be built, hired the team at two locations—and I was walking away.

And it wasn't like I was transitioning from one job to the next. I wasn't walking to security. I wasn't leaving on Friday to start a new job on Monday. It was far more uncertain than that. Remember the old adage, "Don't leave a job unless you have a job"?

Yep, that one.

I wasn't necessarily starting a new job. I was walking toward an idea, a possibility at best. When people asked me what I was doing, I didn't have the security of saying, "I'm going to work for _____." My answer would take a little longer than that. "Well, so, you know . . ."

And as I found myself trying to meander through my description, the fear would get a little louder. *If you can't quickly describe what you're doing, how is this going to work?* And for good measure, *By the way, no one makes a career change like this in their midfifties.* And to pile it on . . . *Oh, and did you forget that there's a global pandemic going on?*

What was next for me, according to fear, was failure. But fear wasn't the only voice chiming in. Its distant cousin, constant uncertainty, had a few things to say as well. Not to mention his twin brother, doubt.

But through it all—through the fear, uncertainty, and doubt—there was something else, something deep, something invisible that kept whispering . . .

What's next is worth it.

This is my story of finding what's next. But this isn't a memoir. My hope is to help you find your next. After hearing my story, I hope you'll be better equipped to embrace the emotions, the change, the fear, and to get through it stronger, braver, better.

The truth is, there are some things you'll never know or experience until you open your hands and let go.

That said, this isn't a manifesto demanding that you

leave where you are. It's more of an invitation to join a group of people who feel a mixture of restlessness and hope. We're restless because we feel there's more inside us that has yet to be released. We're hopeful because we're holding on to the thought that our best days are ahead.

If that's you, if you find yourself searching for what's next, trying to discover it, unsettled where you are, welcome to the community.

Or maybe what's next found you. You were suddenly, unexpectedly shown the door, asked to leave, and your next season was thrust upon you. That's so hard, and so tough. You just need to know there's no rejection here. I'm glad you found this book. You are not alone.

What I've discovered is that while our circumstances may be different, much of the emotions are the same. What to do next is scary and comes with a large dose of uncertainty.

But trust me. You can figure this out. We can figure this out, together. That's why I wrote this book.

What I didn't know when I left my job that September is that millions upon millions of people would have their own story of leaving and trying to find what's next. In fact, that's the second thing I would tell myself in the Elon Musk–induced time-travel conversation.

Learn all you can and pass it along. There are people just as nervous and excited and sad and intrigued and worried and courageous to find what's next. Use your story to help theirs.

And that's my hope for this book. I want these pages to give you practical and proven advice. I want these pages to encourage you, maybe provoke you to get moving, to help you determine when it's time to leave, or determine how much longer you should stay. We're going to talk about managing risk, discovering the strongest version of you, and how to build a life you enjoy. Most of all, I want these pages to help you take a step.

Just. Keep. Walking.

You see, what to do next requires movement, change, and for you to fill a larger space than where you are right now.

No, it won't be easy. But we didn't sign up for easy; we signed up for worthwhile.

And here's what I know. If you'll do the work, keep walking, show up each day, eventually, inevitably, not only will you find what to do next. What to do next will find you.

It's this surprising mystery. There's so much you don't know that is headed your way. It's one of the many reasons this photo is important to me. And, honestly, sobering.

This is moments before we got in our car and drove away on that final day at Gwinnett Church, a final day of that season of certainty. We had just crossed the finish line.

Part of me wants to tell the guy in the photo to *buckle up*. A lot of emotions, change, hurt, worry, and confusion are headed his way. (I'm not going to lie to you. Figuring out what to do next is hard.)

But most of all, I would want to tell him there's an idea coming that he can't see at the moment. There's a group of people who are where he is with the same doubts, fears, hopes, and similar dreams.

Get in the car and drive away, I would tell him.

Looking back, I've discovered once again that what's next is worth it. After all, look at where it led me. It led me to you. You're reading this book. You're a part of what's next for me. And I'm a part of what's next for you.

How crazy, wonderful, and mysterious is that?

And so I wonder. *Where will your best next step lead you? To whom will your best next step lead you?*

This book is an invitation. Yes, we've got bills to pay. Yes, we need to lean into a process. And yes, the emotions that come with all of this are real.

But don't forget the mystery, the wonder, and the possibility of what happens when you move in faith, courage, and hope to find what's next. Because one day, you'll look back on a photo like this and realize there was so much that hung in the balance of your decision to find what's next.

That said, we've got work to do.

We need to get started.

It's time to turn the page.

CHAPTER 1

Knowing When to Leave

Let's wind the clock back two years before that photo was taken on that last day in September 2020. I was meeting with my personal advisory board (more on this later). As is often the case with these guys, a simple question changed my perspective.

"In a couple of years, you and Wendy will become empty nesters," one of my advisors said. "Have you thought about that season and what you would want to do next?"

"Honestly, no."

"Well, now's the time," he said. It was that simple, and that hard.

Where do you begin trying to figure out something as big and massive as a life change? How do you start? How long is this going to take?

It's hard and uncomfortable answering questions that

seemingly have no easy answers. It's why Netflix was created. It's easier to just binge-watch our discomfort away.

What? A new season of Virgin River *is on. I'll figure out the rest of my life later.*

As the old adage says, "Life is what happens when you're trying to figure out what to do with your life."

Answering questions that seem to have no easy answer are why, if you'll allow me, I want to be on your personal advisory board. This book has the assessment and strategies to help guide you to find the answers to your "what's next?" questions.

And yes, it's going to take work.

We're going to build your network. We're going to scale the money wall. We're going to assess the risk of you leaving or staying. I'm going to show you how to get started on your next season, and how to arrive prepared.

We're also going to do some internal work, because life is not only about what to do next; it's also about who you are becoming in the process. Actually, who you're becoming is *more important*. Buckle up, we've got some hard but helpful self-care coming up.

Along the way, I'll be available for you to text with a question or thought. I'll share my cell phone number in just a little while.

Most of all, as you consider hard-to-answer questions

like the ones I faced, you just need to know you're not alone.

We're a people in transition. I wrote this book in the summer and fall of 2021, a time of incredible transition in our country. During one month that summer, four million people quit their jobs in America.[1]

That's right. One month. Four million.

Some economists described this season as The Great Resignation. Others called it Resignation Nation. Either way you look at it, that's four million people in one month walking toward what's next. I'm not sure why. There are probably four million different reasons. But they all woke up the next day wondering the same thing: *What's next?*

And there's a challenge to all of this. What to do next is a hard thing to figure out. This season often arrives with lots of questions and few answers. Like when my personal advisory board challenged me. You'll think things like this:

How do I know whether I should stay or leave?
How do I know the difference between fear and wisdom?
How much risk is too much risk?
How do I balance my dreams with the fact that I need health insurance?
How many times will I wake up in the middle of the

night and think, Oh no! What have I done?
(Spoiler alert: A LOT.)
What do I do now?
Where do I start?

What to do next isn't about mere external details though. Sometimes it's an internal war. Insecurities—which are often kept at arm's length through a season of certainty—are now within punching distance. A comment here, a news story there, a disappointing circumstance—and you're suddenly knocked down.

All of us have been there. The secret is having the courage, stamina, vision, and energy to get back up. We're going to develop these traits together.

When life knocks you down, there's a secret to getting back up—you know what's next. You see it, even if it's faint and dim. You can see it.

And if you can't see it yet, that's okay. It's why I appointed myself to be on your personal advisory board.

Let's get started.

Years ago, I heard a sermon from a pastor named A. L. Patterson about a man named Shamgar in the Bible. You can google it.[2] It will be worth your time. Here are his three points:

1. Start where you are.
2. Use what you have.
3. Do what you can.

In many ways, this is the pathway to what's next.

Max De Pree writes, "The first responsibility of a leader is to define reality."[3] This advice is not just true for leaders. In order to make your way forward, you must be honest with where you've been, how you got to where you are now, and what you can leverage to discover what's next. If you're not careful, you can take for granted where you are and what you have at your disposal. This is why "start where you are"—defining your reality—is so important.

To help clearly define your reality, I created the Career Risk Assessment.

Now, don't let this scare you. It's not a pass/fail grade. The Career Risk Assessment is simply an assessment to help you see where you are so you can start where you are.

Here's how it works.

The Career Risk Assessment will take you through a series of questions. You'll be asked about your sense of happiness and purpose. Other questions focus on your saving and spending habits. A few questions are about your strengths and weaknesses in your job. All of this will assess the amount of risk you'll face if you were to make a career change. Calculating your current level of risk is a great way to "start where you are."

This simply means looking at the cold, hard facts of where you are financially, emotionally, and vocationally. The good news is that the facts aren't always cold and hard. They are actually a gift. Facts are not there to discourage you; facts are there to inform you. Every finish line has a starting line. In fact, the starting line provides direction toward the finish line. That's the power of starting where you are.

Once you have completed the Career Risk Assessment, you'll receive a red light, yellow light, or green light.

A red light doesn't mean failure. Neither does a green light mean go.

A red light means you have work to do before making a significant change. For example, you may need to focus on increasing your financial margin, or you may need to start building your network of personal contacts. A green light means you've positioned yourself for what's next, but it doesn't mean you have to go. With a green light, you're often looking for consensus among people you trust. If the right opportunity or idea hasn't arrived, the most important and hardest decision is to be patient. (In an upcoming chapter, we're going to talk about what to do while you wait.) And finally, a yellow light doesn't mean slow down. A yellow light, in our case, means keep moving but continue to put yourself in a position to reduce the risk of stepping into what's next. An example of this would be a side-hustle, which we'll talk about soon.

The Career Risk Assessment won't make the decision for you. It will give you insights to make the best decision possible.

As you read this, you may be saying, "Jeff, it's a little too late. I quit my job last week."

I get it. But that's why the Career Risk Assessment will be even more helpful. It will show you the work you need to do right away. You just may need more speed than before.

Either way, here's our first big step on the journey to knowing what's next.

Visit JeffHenderson.com, click on Assessments, and then on Career Risk Assessment. Take a few minutes and discover where you are. It's free. It will only take a few minutes. And did I mention it's free?

If you're not going to do this and just keep reading, please understand this: Action > Worrying.

Too often, we are paralyzed by worry and fear. The

antidote isn't certainty—who has 100 percent certainty of anything? The antidote is action.

Take action. Take the Career Risk Assessment. You can't "start where you are" until you are "honest with where you are."

One of the most significant moments in my journey toward what's next came six weeks after I left the church. I was speaking at an event hosted by one of my mentors, John Maxwell. John opened the conference by sharing something I will never forget.

"I never had a clear vision," John said. "I just kept moving forward."

Wait. I get the fact that I don't have a clear, exact vision of what's next for me. I'm a mere mortal. But John Maxwell? *The* leadership guru? John didn't invent leadership, but in many ways he invented the leadership category. He has sold a gazillion books and has spoken all around the world, and yet he didn't have a clear vision?

John knew he had a calling to help leaders. He just didn't know exactly how it was going to play out.

So he refused to get stuck. He simply took massive action. He kept moving.

You and I—let's choose to do the same. Let's keep moving. We can't get stuck in regret, worry, or fear. We need to keep moving.

The Comparison Scoreboard

Can I tell you a secret? I've often felt like I'm behind in life. I don't know why. It just feels like I should be farther along by now. Often, it's the comparison game many of us play:

I should be married by now. Most of my friends are.
I should have x amount of dollars in the bank by now.
Look at where this person is in their career and look at
    where I am.

The comparison game comes with a clock and a scoreboard. In fact, let me ask you a fairly challenging question: If you are playing the comparison game, who's on the other side of the scoreboard? Who are you playing against?

The more points they put on the board, the farther you feel behind. It's why this is such a dangerous game to play. When we compare ourselves to others, we're actually limiting ourselves. We are allowing their success to define the win. My friend Tim Tassopoulos, president and COO of Chick-fil-A, has often reminded me, "Don't compare yourself to others; compare yourself to your potential."

When we feel like we're way behind in life and that others are farther ahead, what to do next begins to grow into an insurmountable obstacle with no hope of overcoming. We look up at this mountain and we're already tired. When we compare ourselves to our potential, the scoreboard is still there, but it's a far healthier and more enjoyable one.

Can I add something to this that I think will help? It may be hard to believe, and I'm not trying to discount your current reality. But this truth may just make the climb seem less daunting. Ready?

You're not behind.

Let's read it again.

You're not behind.

In fact, this time, say it out loud: "I'm not behind."

How can I possibly say this without knowing your story? Because what is behind you is part of your unique story. When you understand your story isn't part of a comparison game, and that the details of your life are not tallied on some comparison scoreboard, it releases some of the pressure.

What's behind you has shaped you, good and bad. What's behind you becomes *dangerous* when it shackles you. What's behind you becomes *helpful* when you embrace where you are as a starting point, not a conclusion. It's why you need to become less judgmental about yourself and much more curious about yourself.

What's behind you becomes *helpful* when you embrace where you are as a starting point, not a conclusion.

Often, we are our own worst critics. We beat ourselves up, hold ourselves down, and lock ourselves in. Instead, let's become more curious. Let's ask questions like this:

How did I get here?
What are strengths of mine that I have leveraged?
What are strengths that have gone dormant that I
    need to revive?
What is holding me back?
Who is holding me back?

Again, this is why the Career Risk Assessment can be so helpful. Did you notice that we didn't compare you to someone else? It's not about them; it's about you.

And yet, if you take the role of a judge, you'll see this assessment as a critique, not a guide. Don't go there.

Take the assessment. Take in the results. And think of the next step as more of a discovery process. More curiosity, less conclusions.

But Seriously, How Did You Know?

One of the most frequent questions I get nowadays is, "How did you know? How did you know it was time to make a career change?"

And then there's usually a pause.

". . . during a global pandemic?"

While this was the first time I had made a career change during a pandemic, I've made my share of career changes before, and each came with plenty of risk. You can't make changes in life without encountering some sort of risk, especially when it comes to career changes.

If you're looking for a risk-free life, I'm not sure you'll find it. There's good news though. You can't eliminate risk, but you can reduce it. Trust me. I know all about it.

You can't eliminate risk, but
you can reduce it.

I've made my share of career changes that could be described as risky—none bigger perhaps than when I left the corporate marketing department at Chick-fil-A in 2003 to join a small team that was launching a video church called Buckhead Church.

I remember Wendy and me trying to explain this to my parents. "I'm leaving a multibillion-dollar company to help launch a church where the preacher is on video."

Blank stares.

Again, you can't eliminate risk but you can manage it. And you manage risk by shrinking it.

Think of it this way. A career change doesn't have to be a leap over the Grand Canyon. It can be managed to be more like a leap over a mud puddle. Sure, you might not make it and you'll get wet and muddy in the process, but you won't plunge thousands of feet below.

There was a strong possibility that Buckhead Church wouldn't work. After all, video church? Really? So I decided to shrink the risk gap. Here's how we did that.

1. **Manage the financial risk.** More on this later, but Wendy and I had done the hard work to get our financial lives ready if and when our best next step appeared.

2. **Value your relationships.** When I left Chick-fil-A, I wrote everyone in the marketing department and on the executive leadership team a handwritten

note thanking them for their friendship and support. I also let them know I would still represent Chick-fil-A very well as an unofficial staff person from this point forward. I ended up writing nearly one hundred notes. While each note was a sincere expression of thanks, it also had a subtle message: "If Buckhead Church doesn't work out, can I come back?"

3. **Know your strengths.** It was clear that the role I was going to have at Buckhead Church was in line with my strengths and gifts. This is one of the most tangible ways to eliminate the risk. You usually do something good when you're good at something.

You usually do something good
when you're good at something.

I'm often asked, "Did you know that Buckhead Church was going to work?" While I understand the question, there's actually a better one: "Was Buckhead Church worth the risk?" Wendy and I were in complete agreement. One thousand percent it was. We weren't sure how it would work out; we just knew the path would be worth following.

Knowing When to Take the Leap

I'm always looking for confirmation when I'm making decisions. Maybe it's my natural insecurity. But I was given a statement confirming that if I had to choose between early or late, it's better to choose too early when it comes to making the leap toward what's next: "I would rather leave a year too early than a day too late."

This statement came to me during lunch with my friend, James Merritt. Dr. Merritt is the senior pastor of Cross Pointe Church in Atlanta. He graciously allowed us to help launch Gwinnett Church on Sunday nights at Cross Pointe in 2012. We were there for three years and became good friends in the process.

It didn't hurt that we were both alumni of the University of Georgia. On our last Sunday at Cross Pointe, I presented Dr. Merritt with a UGA football helmet. That may not seem like a big deal to you, but then again, maybe you didn't graduate from Georgia. It was the perfect gift.

A few years later, he gave me the gift of that quote about leaving too early or too late. This isn't a call for a reckless decision; it's more of a reminder that you'll never truly be ready.

As the Clash sang back in the 1980s, "Should I stay or

should I go?"[4] Great question, but when you ask it for too long, wisdom can turn it into fear.

Risk is inevitable, but so is reward when we manage the risk. Sometimes the riskiest decision isn't to leave. Sometimes the riskiest decision is to stay.

The Gift of Not Knowing

I've never really known what my dream job should be.

With the exception of knowing that I wanted to play in the National Basketball Association. That I knew. The closest I got to the NBA was my friendship with Mark Price, the legendary Cleveland Cavalier.

Other than that, I've never really "known."

I envy those who do. Maybe that's you, so I officially envy you. Perhaps you grew up knowing you would be a doctor, teacher, lawyer, parent, and so forth. I was always guessing. There were clues as I look back now, but I never really knew. The plan just slowly came into focus for me. All these years later, I'm in my dream job for the moment. But I've discovered something about dream jobs. There's more than one. Again, at least for me.

I loved working in sports marketing at Chick-fil-A. After all, part of my job was watching college football to make sure the Chick-fil-A commercials aired during the broadcast. "Can't cut the grass today, honey. Gotta see if our commercials are running during the game." Tough job, but somebody's gotta do it.

I loved launching three churches in my hometown of Atlanta, even though as a preacher's kid myself, I swore I'd never work at a church.

And as uncertain as these early days are, I love my current dream job of starting my own company with Wendy and friends.

Along the way, I've discovered an important truth about these dream jobs that I think can be both helpful and encouraging. The path to your dream job often leads through your day job. (More on this later as well.)

What propelled you into your day job is often a clue to something hidden within you. Too often though, we can be dismissive of our day job. One more day here is one day longer than we want. But we do ourselves a disservice when we dismiss our day job completely. If we look more closely and show up each day ready to give our best, we'll often see a trail of clues and experience a strong, connected network of people around us.

The path to your dream job often leads through your day job.

It's why not knowing what to do next can be a blessing.

It forces us to leverage what's currently in front of us to figure out what's ahead of us. To borrow A. L. Patterson's words, "Use what you have."

I can tell you this. When we focus on what we don't have instead of being a good steward of what we do have, we will rarely be led to a dream job of any sort. That said, let's take stock of what we do have.

1. **People.** Some call this a network, and one of the best ways to find what's next is found here. This is why the LinkedIn social networking site is such a gift. Start following people. Comment on their posts. Send them a direct message. After a while, ask them for advice.

2. **Experience.** Don't discount your experience, even in the mundane. If you've helped a business or organization thrive, you have a story to share. If you're seeking to get hired, it's helpful to show that you think like an owner, not an employee. You understand how an organization works. You helped make a business more profitable because of the way you paid attention to the health of the business. You weren't just clocking in; you were showing up.

What I've discovered is that not knowing what we

should do next can be an exciting, mysterious journey. When we do the hard work of this chapter, life tends to show up, reward our work, and point the way. It's what happened one fateful day for me in Chicago in 1998.

I was attending a leadership conference on a beautiful August day in a suburb of Chicago. (Warning: Be very wary of visiting Chicago in August. It tricks you into thinking winter won't come.) I was working at Chick-fil-A at the time and was there with several people from the marketing department. Little did I know that this conference would arrange a meeting between what's next and me.

On the second day at a break, I walked over to the lake behind the church by myself. It's hard to describe what happened next, only to say I had some sort of spiritual experience. This is a business book, so for those of you who are starting to get nervous, hang with me. This won't be long. And I do have a point for all of us.

I didn't hear anything. I didn't see anything. And yet I did hear something, and I did see something. (See, I told you it was hard for me to describe.) I heard a calling. I saw a calling. It sounded like this: "You're going to start a church someday."

Okay, I'll stop there. But here's my point. While in Chicago, I didn't go looking for what to do next. What I would do next came looking for me.

And yet the work I had done put me in a position to be

in Chicago. That's the gift of not knowing but still doing the work. This is what I'm inviting you into, no matter where you are on the journey to what's next. Don't get paralyzed by the uncertainty. Embrace the mystery.

You're on the front end of one of the great stories in your one and only life. Think of it as a movie script. You've been given the starring role, and the conflict in the story is how you're going to move through this season better, stronger, braver. A better, stronger, braver you is a great gift to your world. If you won't do it for you, do it for us.

Knowing I had a greater opportunity to serve others is also what helped me shrink the gap of risk. Anytime I felt afraid about leaving Chick-fil-A for church planting, which was pretty much all the time, I remembered the work. I remembered Chicago. I remembered the people I could serve and lead in the meantime.

It gave me the confidence to just keep walking. And when you keep walking, one day you'll know.

All of which takes me back to the original idea of this chapter: *knowing when to leave*. First, if you've made it this far in the book, it's a sign you're closer than you may think. The clock is ticking. You've defined where you are, which is a strong step. The next step is to look two enemies squarely in the eye—fear and risk—and ask yourself a good question: "Is it time?"

CHAPTER 2

Is It Time to Make a Change?

One of the more humorous conversations leading up to my departure from Gwinnett Church was with my ninety-four-year-old mom.

You would love my mom, by the way. A few years ago, when she was eighty-nine, she met Tim Tebow, and her reaction was so epic it went viral. Even TMZ picked it up, making my mom the first eighty-nine-year-old to be featured on that show. She was also featured in *Sports Illustrated*. I grew up reading *Sports Illustrated* and wanting to get my name in it someday. I never imagined my mom would beat me to it.

If you want to see the epic moment, just search "89-year-old grandmother meets Tim Tebow." You'll thank me later. Her next goal is to meet Trae Young of the Atlanta Hawks. Get ready, TMZ.

Back to the more pressing issue about what to do next.

I've discovered that no matter how old you get, you still have to explain these decisions to your mother. In my case, I had to explain to my mom why I was leaving my full-time job at Gwinnett Church and what I was intending to do.

I'm the son of a preacher man. Ministry runs in our blood. Explaining to my mom why I was stepping down as a pastor and stepping into something new, undefined—the idea of a new company—well, let's just say I was nervous.

For a woman in her nineties, my mom is in great health. She can't hear very well, though, so I have to raise my voice when I speak with her. If you ever see us having dinner at a restaurant, I assure you I'm not yelling at my mom. She just can't hear me. It's why I thought a visual would help me explain.

When we launched the FOR Gwinnett idea at Gwinnett Church—an idea where churches are known more for what they are FOR than what they're against—it quickly caught on in places around the country and the world. Organizations started sending me T-shirts and coffee mugs to say thanks, highlighting the simple, powerful message of FOR.

FOR Guatemala. FOR El Paso. FOR Chicago. FOR Dubai. And on and on.

I decided to bring these shirts to her house as a visual prop to explain why I was starting an organization called the FOR Company. I wanted to help these organizations shrink the gap between what they want to be known FOR and what they are known FOR.

With about twenty T-shirts as my props in her small kitchen, I did my best to explain what Wendy and I had decided to do next. After a few moments of silence, my mom asked, "You're moving to Guatemala?"

Here's something you need to know about what's next: not everyone will get it—and that's okay.

While I sought my mom's blessing, which she eventually gave me, she still isn't quite sure what I'm doing.

Heck, some days *I'm* not even sure.

If you're looking for a sure thing before you move, you probably won't move. It's why we need to spend some time talking about risk. The risk with what's next is almost always apparent and easy to identify; the risk with staying usually hides. There is risk on both sides.

Sometimes the biggest risk isn't leaving; sometimes the biggest risk is staying.

Sometimes the biggest risk isn't leaving;
sometimes the biggest risk is staying.

How do you know which risk is greater? Like anything in life, you get to work. As your self-appointed personal advisory board member, I want to show you how. You can't eliminate risk but you can manage it. By doing so, you can find your best next step. Maybe more importantly, it can show those closest to you that you aren't being unwise—you've actually done the work.

And maybe the most important person who will feel some relief is you. You can sleep better at night knowing you've put in the work to eliminate any unnecessary risk. That's what this chapter is all about—managing risk and getting better sleep. Now that's a win-win.

Define Your Risk

The first step is to come face-to-face with your specific risk. Often, our risk is like a middle school bully that pushes us around and takes our lunch money. When we finally have the courage to stand up for ourselves, we find that the bully isn't as strong as we thought. When I was in the seventh grade, a fellow student bullied me around for most of the school year. Years later, I ran into this guy. I was five inches taller than him, and the whole time we were talking, I was wondering, *How could I have ever been afraid of this guy?*

So I beat him up.

I'm just kidding, people.

Once you have the courage to go face-to-face with the

risk bully, you'll often ask, *What took me so long to stand up for myself?* The first step toward standing up is to print out your results of the Career Risk Assessment. Each result—red, yellow, or green—will provide three specific action items. And yes, we're going old school by printing things out. I even want you to tape the results on your bathroom mirror.

Each morning and night, I want you to see the work you need to do. It's not an exhaustive list, but remember, you're not trying to figure out the rest of your life. You're just trying to move from one light to the next. That's all. Moving may take longer than you think, but once you're done, you'll think, *Well, that didn't take too long. I should have beat up that bully a long time ago.*

On the other hand, you don't *have* to move on to the next score. You can worry, fret, or complain instead—in other words, nothing that's really helpful. Or you can get working, focusing on the progress you need to make. As John Maxwell says, "What you focus on expands."[5]

I want you to expand your opportunities by focusing on moving from one color score to the next. From red light to yellow light. From yellow light to green light. From green light to what's next.

I want you to expand your future by focusing on generating positive momentum. I want you to expand your potential by focusing more on your gifts and strengths. This focus will expand your *opportunities* and lead to something you may not currently have—momentum.

It's why quick wins matter. I call it a quick win, not a small win, because there's nothing small about it. Something really big is happening with a quick win. When you work through the steps, you will get some quick wins. For example, if you received a red light, one quick win is to ask four people one specific question. Another win will be a quick financial step to take. There are similar quick wins with both yellow and green lights as well.

These wins are going to create real momentum. It may be the first sense of momentum you've experienced in quite a while.

If you're married, there are additional benefits to following through on the action steps from the assessment. Each completed step can eliminate arguments you may have about what's next, because now you have a clear plan. When we're considering a change in our career, there's often too much emotion and not much of a plan. Also, usually in a marriage, one spouse is more comfortable with risk than the other. If your spouse is less comfortable with risk than you are, the assessment results will be a huge value-add to them. The results will show them there's a plan with clear next steps.

Here's what I predict will happen as you start to make plans for what to do next, based on your assessment results. You're going to be pleasantly surprised. You're going to have a conversation with someone that leads to something. You're going to take new ground financially. You're going to gain clarity on how your gifts will lead you to your future. Something will happen along the way.

It's mysterious, yes. I would suggest spiritual, but either way, I believe the work you put in to move from one level of risk to the next will be rewarded.

Instead of trying to figure out what to do for the rest of your life, do something that will involve the next month or quarter. Sure, it may even take longer than that, but taking the assessment and considering your score are two ways to put yourself in the best possible place for growth.

The hardest part about figuring out what to do next may be taking the very first step.

Let's take it.

Without a first step, we stay where we are.

Get out of Your Head, and Then out of Your Way

One of my favorite quotes from Donald Miller's book *Business Made Simple* is this: "Nothing will cost you more in life than a predetermined belief that things aren't going to work out."[6]

I couldn't agree more. The power of working a plan is it gets us out of our way. It gets us moving. It gets us out of our head where all the doubts and insecurities swirl. Fear doesn't do well with movement. It's better at paralyzing us with inaction. Figuring out what to do next requires action.

Remember the pathway to what's next:

1. Start where you are.
2. Use what you have.
3. Do what you can.

You're going to start where you are—red, yellow, or green. You're going to use what you have, and you now have something you didn't have a few days ago—an assessment with a solid plan. You're going to do what you can to take your best next step, because one step forward is one step closer.

In the pages ahead, we're going to make that solid plan even stronger while also instilling a growing belief that, yes, things indeed are going to work out.

They're going to work out just fine. Who knows? You may even move to Guatemala.

The Fast Track Is Slower Than You Think (and That's a Good Thing)

If this were a movie, I would discover the answer to what's next about a week after my personal advisory board meeting. Sometimes that happens.

Sometimes.

But my experience is that what's next likes to hide.

Not only does it seem so mysterious, playing some cruel game of hide-and-seek, but next is also so s . . . l . . . o . . . w.

Why does it take so long? Why is this such a slow process? Life seems to be flying by, and we seem to be stuck. It's why we have to remember that figuring out what to do next is a process.

In my case, it took two years of conversations, thinking, observation, prayer, and more conversations to determine that next had finally arrived. And yet, even then, it still seemed mysterious. As I mentioned in the very beginning, I wasn't leaving for a new job as much as I was walking toward an idea, a possibility. And it's hard to deposit possibility in the bank.

But that moment with my personal board of advisors was a wake-up call. It put me on notice, but it didn't cause me to panic.

Little did I know at the time that the journey I was about to embark on would lead me to you in the hope that I could help you find out what's next.

I want to take you back to that meeting with my board of advisors who gave me a fantastic piece of advice for figuring out what's next: *pay attention to where the momentum is.*

Pay attention to where the momentum is.

This advice was a game changer for me. It turned me into an investigator, not a judge. A judge, as I mentioned earlier, isn't very helpful with what's next. A judge offers rulings and decisions. An investigator, on the other hand, is looking for clues.

As you consider what to do next, get in the habit of looking for clues of momentum. Be an investigator of your own life. Looking for clues of momentum helps guide you, lead you. It whispers, *Come over here.*

At the time I received this advice, I was a few months away from releasing *Know What You're FOR*—a business book that provides two questions to help organizations and leaders grow.

I wanted to test out whether the content would resonate with business leaders, so I created a tour around the country called the "Business Breakfast Tour." I eventually visited twenty-five cities—from San Francisco to St. Louis to Charlotte to Athens, Georgia, to places in between. (Shout-out to Elkhorn, Nebraska, tour stop #5!)

At these tour stops, I gave a one-hour presentation about the content of the book. I approached this tour as an investigator, asking, "Is there momentum here?"

Long story short, there was.

Tour stop after tour stop, I spoke with business owners, managers, and teams and got direct feedback about the content. I remember telling Wendy, "There's momentum with the FOR book that I think we need to pay attention to."

To put this in Career Risk Assessment terms, we had arrived at a yellow light. Again, in our terminology, yellow isn't bad. It means move cautiously but confidently until you get a green light.

In our case, it meant keep going. Those business breakfasts were leading somewhere. There was momentum there.

All of this leads to a question: *Where are you seeing momentum in your life?* It's hard to see momentum in our own lives. I get that. This isn't the moment for humility as much as it is for honesty.

I've had people tell me there's no momentum in their lives, and yet they have a contact list of people that would make all of us envious. Their momentum is their personal network. Others have momentum in their family life. Others have a healthy cash margin set aside to explore what's next. Others may have momentum in their spiritual or physical life.

Either way, that momentum is a clue. As my advisory board told me, "Pay attention to where the momentum is." Fuel it. Stoke it. Keep it going.

Momentum takes all sorts of different forms, and sometimes it isn't an outward example we can point to, such as a book tour. Sometimes the most important momentum we create is internal by working on a healthier version of us, whether emotionally, relationally, physically, or spiritually.

Sometimes when what's next arrives and we aren't emotionally healthy, what's next becomes more of a curse than a blessing. This is why I tell younger leaders, "The fast track is slower than you think"—which is usually received with the same response to "give me twenty-five push-ups." No one likes to hear something like that—except maybe Jocko Willink.

And yet it's heartbreaking when I see people who aren't ready for what's next. They think they can run a marathon on a week's worth of training.

For example, we've all heard stories of people who started a job three months ago and are now wondering, *Why haven't I gotten a promotion yet?*

Here's some good news and bad news:

You can't fast-track character.
You can't fast-track experience.
You can't fast-track growth.

The best form of momentum is a more emotionally healthy you. In fact, the more emotionally healthy you are, the better investigator you will become because you can spot the momentum in your life easier.

You can't microwave character, endurance, persistence, and grit.

Discovering what's next is tied to who you are becoming in the process.

Your personal momentum, or lack thereof, will ultimately determine how much overall momentum you'll experience. In fact, I've got some great news if you have no clue what's next: *You've been given more time to create more personal momentum.*

And when we get healthier as people, we ultimately find our way. Sure, the fast track may be slower than we think, but once we're there, we go farther than we could imagine.

The Law of the Lid

Eventually, it came down to a choice. I could stay where I was, at a place I loved, but there would be a cost. It became clear there would be no future growth for me. And yet I knew there was more I could offer—not from a prideful standpoint, but from a stewardship standpoint.

I believe I'll stand before God someday and give an account of my life. When we get to this point of my story and I'm asked, "So you hit a lid in your career. What did you do next?" I didn't want my answer to be, "Well, I just gave up, put my head down, and stayed where I was. After all, I had to have insurance."

In the grand expanse of eternity, that's not a great answer. That would be on me, not anyone else.

Ultimately, you and I are responsible for stewarding our gifts and talents. And when you hit a lid like I did, even though it's frustrating, it can actually be a gift.

I was discussing this with one of my advisors, who told me, "One of the best ways to view a no in the present is to see it as a yes for your future. You've got clarity. There's no future for you here. But it doesn't mean there's not a future. Your future just opened up."

John Maxwell talks about the law of the lid.[7] I realized I had hit a lid, and the lid was there to stay. The only way to remove the lid is by growing your leadership ability.

It's why when I'm asked the "should I stay or should I go?" question, I ask, "How much opportunity do you have to grow your gifts, talents, and leadership ability where you are?" That answer alone should bring some clarity. And here's why: *if there's no room to grow, it's time to go.*

> Sidenote: Ultimately, it's not about you and me and our gifts and feeling fulfilled; it's about leveraging our lives in such a way that we are fully where we should be—putting our gifts and talents to use for the betterment of others. You'll always be happiest when you're living your life FOR others.

When the opportunity for growth shrinks, we all lose. We need you fully alive and growing.

If there's no room to grow, it's time to go.

We also need you in a situation that makes you feel like you're in over your head. "New levels bring new devils," as Bishop T. D. Jakes says.[8] New challenges bring out a new you; lids never do.

So take a look around. Have you hit a lid? Have you been given clarity that the lid isn't moving? If so, I think you have your answer.

Write a Great Next Chapter

I'm a big believer in the power of ninety days. A quarter might not change your life, but you can certainly gain momentum with increased focus over this time span.

My friend Tommy Newberry is a bestselling author and success coach. He introduced me to this concept more than twenty years ago when I was working at Chick-fil-A. Near the beginning of a new quarter, I would get together with Tommy and a small group to prepare.

We'd look back on the previous quarter and ask questions such as these:

→ What went well, and why?
→ What didn't go so well, and why?
→ How can we increase momentum in the areas that are going well?
→ What can we do to start momentum in areas that aren't going well?

These gatherings became a refueling station for me. I didn't know how low on fuel I was until I came to these meetings. Life has a tendency to deplete us, right? Being around like-minded people who had big dreams, but often big challenges as well, inspired and rejuvenated me.

I began to see the next ninety days as a blank canvas with one overarching goal: *write a great next chapter over the next quarter.*

That's all. Just write a great next chapter over the next ninety days. I knew that winning the next ninety days would create momentum for the quarter beyond that. The way you win the next ninety days is to have more good days than bad. Ultimately, this is how you write a great story with your life. You write great chapters.

The better days you have, the better weeks you have.

The better weeks you have, the better months you have.

The better months you have, the better quarters you have.

The better quarters you have, the better life you live.

Again, it's that simple. And that hard.

I love this quote from John Wooden: "Be quick—but don't hurry."[9] Be quick on the things you can control, like setting aside time each quarter to review and reflect on the last ninety days while preparing for the upcoming ninety days. But don't hurry yourself into thinking you have to figure out the rest of your life today. Focus on the next ninety days. Write the next great chapter.

To help with this, I've created a free, one-page, half-day work session that will help you write a great next chapter in the upcoming ninety days. Just visit jeffhenderson.com /next90days to access it.

Ideally, you would gather a small group of like-minded people and work through this exercise together. This group could consist of coworkers or friends who both challenge and inspire you and are in a similar season. I've gathered for sessions like this for the past twenty years with my friends David Farmer and Shane Benson. We share our wins and losses, ups and downs, but ultimately we look toward the future—the next ninety days and beyond.

Having a long-term vision combined with a ninety-day implementation plan is a "be quick—but don't hurry" way to live.

This small but important exercise will help you write a great next chapter over the next ninety days. Believe it or not, this simple step will go a long way toward helping you answer the question we're all trying to figure out: *How do you know what's next?*

Write a great chapter over the next ninety days. Be quick—but don't hurry.

Hands in the Air

I've said it before, and I'll write it again: *what's next is hard.*

It feels like being the new kid in school, standing in the lunch line with your tray of food wondering where to sit. You feel alone. Whatever you do next will be like wearing a brand-new pair of shoes—shiny on the outside, blisters a few days later on the inside. That's what new seasons and adventures bring.

While starting the FOR Company and leaving Gwinnett Church isn't the first time I've started over, previous experience never makes the present experience easier. You just have memories, wins and scars reminding you that it's worth it—one of the few advantages those of us who are fifty-plus have over the younger folks.

There's also another word that comes to mind describing what's next: *roller coaster.*

Confession: I'm no fan of roller coasters. Other than speed and heights, I think I would get along fine with them. But since slow and low-to-the-ground roller coasters are fairly nonexistent (or are in the kiddie section of the park), I've decided to keep my distance.

But *roller coaster* certainly has described every new season I've had. And that may be true for you as well.

There was the time a couple of months after I left Gwinnett Church when I had a big in-person speaking engagement coming up in a few days, and I felt like I was getting sick, which led to a mild panic attack. Wendy calmed me down. I ended up speaking, completely healthy, which led to so many other opportunities I'm blessed with today. But those few days, let me tell you—#rollercoaster.

There was another time when a fantastic opportunity appeared out of nowhere. It seemed as though this opportunity would set the direction for much of the rest of the year, only to see it evaporate. I followed my twenty-four-hour rule of grieving disappointments and then got back up when a new, even better opportunity appeared. Again, #rollercoaster.

And there are those times when I woke up afraid in the middle of the night. Very, very afraid. *What if this doesn't work?* The one advantage people have with theme park roller coasters is they see the finish. You know where you are ultimately landing.

That's not necessarily true with what you will do next. Sure, you have a vision. You probably have a clear problem you're trying to help solve. But what you can't foresee are the twists and turns you'll experience.

And while I have no credibility in speaking of theme park roller coasters, there is one experience I've decided to lean in and emulate. I've seen my family and friends do it when they're on a roller coaster. As the ride slowly begins its ascent up the track, the really brave souls lift their hands in the air. Instead of gripping the bar in front of them, they open themselves up to the full ride.

I usually watch my loved ones ride the roller coasters from some comfortable spot nearby. *Why do people do this to themselves?* I wonder as I snack on popcorn and Coca-Cola. And that's when I saw this idea related to what's next: the right position leads to a better decision.

Instead of gripping for control and being knocked off-balance constantly by what you don't know, the right position is to let go and lift your hands in the air. Embrace the roller coaster known as "what's next," because honestly, you and I have very little control anyway.

> **The right position leads to a better decision.**

When we're gripping for control, we close ourselves off. When our hands are in the air, we're positioning ourselves to be fully open to the ride. This always leads to better decisions because we're in a better, more positive frame of mind.

The Right Position Leads to a Better Decision

Here's what lifting our hands in the air looks like, practically speaking, as we move toward what's next:

→ **Welcome the twists and turns, knowing they lead to better stories and a better life.** Sure, some things will go exactly as we've planned

49

and hoped. Some will not. Others are still TBD. Through it all, decide to take on the mindset of an investigator and see where things lead. Resist the temptation to adopt the mindset of a perfectionist. Try to avoid interpreting everything that doesn't go according to plan as a mistake. (The life of a perfectionist is a hard one. After all, when does anything go "exactly as planned"?)

> The goal isn't to have your idea win; the goal is to have the best idea win.

Welcome twists and turns as part of the story. Enjoy the wonder of where it will take you. It's like lifting your hands as you crest over the first hill of the roller coaster.

→ **Choose release over control.** In other words, bring your very best to each and every day, and then release the results to God. This is the pathway I was asked to walk when God made it clear my time at Gwinnett Church had come to a close. I've never been in control. Neither have you. Why pretend now?

→ **Trust your intuition while listening to those you trust.** I remember a meeting I had with my publisher and agent about this book. I was very excited about the content. I believed it could help a lot of people. The publisher agreed but wondered whether the demographic was too narrow. I, on the other hand, believe there is "riches in the niches." The more targeted the demographic, the better.

The reality is that both of us were right. In that moment, as a writer and content creator, I was tempted to fight for my idea. Sometimes that's the right course of action. But I was reminded that day to never let that shut down the creative process and conversation. The goal isn't to have your idea win; the goal is to have the best idea win.

During our Zoom meeting, my agent made a suggestion for the book title. Instantly, I knew he was right. While remaining true to my goal for the content, this decision greatly widened the opportunity to serve more people. This is a great reminder for all of us—we is smarter than me.

→ **Embrace laughter as a business-building strategy.** Many of us tend to take life too seriously. I know I do. Laughter helps me balance this out. So as odd as this may seem, I've made laughter a goal for each day—especially while I'm moving toward what's next. If I get to the end of the day and I haven't had a great laugh, well, there's always Nate

Bargatze's *The Tennessee Kid* on Netflix, which I've watched about seventy-two times.

Laughter reminds us that life is too short to be consumed by details that will ultimately work out. Throw your hands in the air. Laugh your way through.

Ironically, laughter is what I usually see when people walk away from one of those death-defying roller coasters. They just paid to be scared out of their minds by flying through the air on a ride created by an engineer they've never met. How do they know that person can be trusted? What if they skipped class on "Roller Coaster Day" at engineering school? You'll never know—or maybe unfortunately you will.

Nevertheless, people walk away laughing, often hugging the person next to them and going back for more. While you'll never find me in line at the Scream Machine, in a very real sense, I'm there right now as I move toward what's next.

We is smarter than me.

Which leads me back to the question, "How do you know if it's time to make a change?"

When you're willing to let go of the bar and lift your hands in the air—that's when.

Sure, figuring out what to do next is still a journey. There are still risks involved. I'm not suggesting you quit tomorrow or jump recklessly into the next season. In fact, the rest of the book has some practical strategies to consider before taking any steps. What I *am* suggesting is that you open yourself up to the journey. Welcome the twists and turns. Commit to laughing more. Choose release over control. And throw those hands up in the air.

CHAPTER 3

The Waiting Room

Have you ever felt forgotten?

One time, during a doctor's visit, they forgot about me. They led me to a room, shut the door, and never came back. I'm currently writing this from there.

Doesn't life feel like that sometimes? It feels like we've been ushered into a waiting room and simply forgotten. Ever been there? Are you there now? On the journey to what's next you may find yourself in the waiting room.

Waiting is hard and dangerous. It's hard because we feel as though our life has been put on hold. No one likes being put on hold. It's the place of bad music and wasted time. It's dangerous because of what we decide to do, or to not do.

When we find ourselves in the waiting room, we have three paths to choose from.

1. Waiting passively.
2. Waiting recklessly.
3. Waiting actively.

Waiting passively is when we conclude that life is completely out of our control and we can't do anything to move ourselves forward—kind of like being stuck in a doctor's office and thinking you can do nothing about it.

Waiting passively is the land of video games and stacks of pizza boxes. It's where we scroll through everyone else's highlight reel on social media, falling for the illusion that their lives are problem-free while we're stuck in the waiting room. It's a vicious cycle that starts to spiral downward quickly.

This is also the place where our excuses start to cement in our soul.

Waiting recklessly is when our frustration boils over and we leap toward the best available option. We're exhausted from being put on hold, so we hang up and move. I completely understand, but the stories of waiting recklessly are the ones I heard often as a pastor. This kind of waiting can create some deep scars.

Waiting recklessly sounds like, *I'm not getting any*

younger, so I may as well take a chance and walk down the aisle with them. After all, no one's perfect.

Or, *Sure it's a lot of debt, but isn't this how you build your credit?*

It becomes the land of greatest regrets when we realize there can be worse things than waiting.

That's the bad news. The good news is there's another, better option.

Waiting actively is when we combine wisdom, patience, and an intentional plan to leverage this season. There actually is something we should be doing while we wait. It's not the land of passivity; it's not the land of being on hold. It's the land of wisdom.

Wisdom in the waiting room discerns the difference between waiting passively, recklessly, and actively. Think about these statements. Have you ever felt or said any of these?

"I've been forgotten." That's waiting passively.

"It's my turn *now*." That's waiting recklessly.

"I'm being prepared." That's waiting actively.

You haven't been forgotten. You are being prepared. Believing these statements will help you see the waiting room as a gift, not a curse. It will also help lead you to discover what's next.

The Microwave versus the Crock-Pot

We all know things taste better when they simmer for a long time compared to taking a microwave approach. And yet all too often we want our lives to be microwaved so we can just move on.

The waiting room is where we simmer. It's where our greatest change takes place. It's the seasoning, the refining, the long nights of uncertainty, where our character is formed, our values are decided, our souls are shaped.

When we bust out of the waiting room by acting impulsively or recklessly, we forfeit the simmering change that could have been.

Waiting passively squanders the time.

Waiting recklessly forces the time.

Waiting actively leverages the time.

Waiting passively squanders *the time.*
Waiting recklessly forces *the time.*
Waiting actively leverages *the time.*

To *squander* means we don't take advantage of the growth opportunity the waiting room provides. To *force* means we decide it's time, and so we move the season from the slow cooker to the microwave. In other words, we're done. The impulse isn't all bad. *I don't want to be a victim. I don't want to be passive. Let's take some action.*

Those are actually good things. But if we're not careful, we can miss the better option—*waiting actively*.

We aren't sitting quietly in the waiting room, just twiddling our thumbs as we wait to be invited into the exam room. We don't simply endure the process; we grow through the process. Our time in the waiting room does not have to be wasted time.

What to Do in the Waiting Room

We all know stories (correction: we all *have* stories) of being so impatient that we decided to act. Now, I've mentioned a lot about the power of action. There's both wise action and the reckless kind. If we come storming out of the waiting room without a plan, we have the potential to recklessly wreck our lives. On the other hand, if we give up and remain passive, hope starts to fade.

As the old proverb says, "Hope deferred makes the heart sick."[10]

The waiting room is hard on our hearts. It feels like we're stuck in a nondescript room, no door handle on the inside, a television on the wall where we see everyone else moving swiftly through their lives. Life is one big smile as one dream after another comes true.

That television, by the way, is called Instagram. And

be careful of what you see. Far too often, Instagram just shows the highlight reels without the drama.

In fact, one of the best strategies to implement in a season of waiting is to cut way back on your time watching Instagram TV. You've been created to live *your* life, not someone else's life. One of the many dangers of the waiting room is that hope can fade and comparison can seep into your heart. I don't want that for you. Heck, *you* don't want that for you.

Instead, I want to give you a principle to hold on to during this season of waiting, along with some practical strategies I've implemented in my own life that I'm confident can help you.

First, I want you to write down this principle somewhere and refer to it often: *don't let what you don't know rob you of what you can do.*

Don't let what you don't know rob you of what you can do.

To wait actively is to understand there are things we don't know. There are reasons for waiting that we can't see right now. The best things take time. It's not all on us. We can choose to be present while still being hopeful for the future.

I mentioned that waiting is hard. Isn't that one of the more ironic aspects of waiting? It's exhausting to do nothing.

And yet don't forget the message from A. L. Patterson:

→ Start where you are.
→ Use what you have.
→ Do what you can.

When we use what we have and do what we can, it's amazing how much of a gift a season of waiting can be. You haven't been forgotten; you are being prepared. Here's how to cooperate with the process and grow in the process.

Step #1: Build Your Network

Your net worth largely depends on your network. It's true—who you know is often more important than what you know. This is why building your personal network is one of the best decisions you can make while you search for what's next.

A network is simply the people in your circle of relationships. What I've discovered is that the person you need to meet is closer than you think. It's the "Six Degrees of Kevin Bacon" game. Apparently, we are just six people away from being able to ask Kevin about *Footloose*.

Because who you know is more important than what you know, coffee with someone you know is always better than sending your résumé to someone you don't. One of the best ways to know what's next is to talk to people you know.

Most of us, though, discount our network. Since we don't know the CEO of a big company, we tend to overlook the manager of a smaller company. And yet, if there's any truth to the theory of six degrees of separation (the real-life theory on which the Kevin Bacon game is based),[11] you're closer to the CEO than you may think.

The bigger problem, though, as it always is, happens to be insecurity. *Why would this person want to meet with me?*

Good news. You've come to the right place. Not only will most of the people you ask agree to meet with you, but they'll be grateful for the time spent with you. And I'm going to give you the perfect questions to ask to build your network.

Remember this: what to do next is built largely on *who* you talk to next.

> **What to do next is built largely on *who* you talk to next.**

If you want to build your net worth, you need to build your network. Here's how:

1. Write Down Every Name You Can Think Of in Your Personal Network

This exercise is critical for starting right where we are. I don't want this to be a haphazard exercise. We're going to take fifteen minutes and do it right. Set your watch, alarm, or timer for fifteen minutes. Then write down every name you can think of in your network. If you can't think of a name, write, "I can't think of a name to write down." (Or write down "Kevin Bacon." You're just six degrees from him anyway.)

The goal is to keep writing. Don't stop. Quantity is far better than quality right now. Just write.

Who do you know? Write it down. If you're wondering whether you should write down a certain person's name, the answer is yes. The more names, the better. (Please understand that most people never do this. As a result, they never truly leverage their personal network.)

2. Rank the Names in Order of Priority

After the fifteen minutes is up, I want you to take two next steps:

1. Circle the names you know the best.
2. Rank the names with great influence in your network, starting at #1—signifying the greatest influence.

"What's the difference?" you ask. Great question.

On the one hand, the names you circle are those you've

known the longest or the best. On the other hand, there may be names in your network who have significant influence and who you don't know as well. I want you to create two separate lists so you can see where the circles and the rankings mesh. When someone in your relational circle has a significant influence, it's an indicator of where to start.

For example, you may come across someone who is exactly in your field of interest. You would want to put them high on the list compared to someone in a completely different field. Granted, that person can still be of value based on their life experience and their own network, and we'll eventually get to them.

Let me give you an example. David Salyers, the former vice president of marketing at Chick-fil-A, is someone I would circle because I've known him for more than twenty-five years. I would also rank him highly as a person of significant influence because of his career and network. And as I've often told David, I want to be like him when I grow up.

The best place to start building your network is where the circles and rankings combine. It's also one of the best ways to wait actively while you're in the waiting room.

3. Let the Contacting Begin

We're now going to begin the networking process. You've developed an initial list and ranked them in terms of when you'll contact them—and now the work begins. Depending on your personality, this next step may seem a bit daunting. It's why I've written out your request for you. Obviously, you decide whether it takes the form of a text, email, phone call, and so forth. But here's what I want you to say:

> Hi, there. I'm in the process of determining my next career move, and I was wondering if you would have twenty minutes for me to hear more of your story. I know there's a lot I can learn from you and what you've done. Would you be willing to meet with me?

Sure, not everyone will say yes, but who knows, maybe they will. What I do know is that most people like sharing their story. You're not asking for a job; you're asking for them to talk about themselves. And most people like talking about themselves. I want you to come with three specific questions:

1. Looking back, what were some of the most helpful strategies that got you to where you are now?
2. What do you know now that you wish you had known ten years ago?
3. What would you do if you were me?

The Best Networking Question Ever

After asking those first three questions, you'll finish with asking the best question I've ever heard when it comes to building your network: *Who do you know that I need to know?* (Shout-out to John Maxwell for teaching me this question.[12] It is flat-out networking gold and worth the price of this book!)

If we were having lunch together, this is when I would stand up, walk around the table, put my hand on your shoulder, and say, "Don't miss this. This question alone is one of the most important ways you'll discover what's next." (And aren't you glad we aren't having lunch together because everyone would wonder what's happening at the table over there where a strange man is putting his hand on the shoulder of that nice person.)

But seriously. On the other side of this question just might be your future.

You're not done yet though. I want you to ask one follow-up question: *Would you be willing to contact them on my behalf?*

They may say no, but I've found it's rare to get that response. People actually feel good when they are helping people, and you're asking for help.

To do this can make us feel very uncomfortable. I get it. I feel the same way.

You know what else makes us uncomfortable? Not getting closer to what's next. You get to pick your discomfort.

As for me, I want to stay in the waiting room as long as it takes for me to grow, but I don't want to stay one second longer than I have to, which is why I'm committed to growing my personal network. It's why I keep reminding myself of this truth: *I'm one person away from the next big opportunity.*

My network largely determines my net worth. The greater my network, the greater my net worth. It's that simple, that uncomfortable, and that promising. Granted, our financial net worth doesn't determine our personal value. But our network does determine how close we move to our potential. In some ways, I wish that weren't true. I wish *what* we know was greater than *who* we know. Sometimes that's true. Yet in the real world, it's all about the network.

You're not running for class president; you're running toward your potential. In fact, you have a stewardship responsibility toward the rest of us. Something inside you needs to be released to the rest of us.

As I wrote in *Know What You're FOR*, it's not about being the best *in* the world; it's about being the best *for* the world. For this to happen, to put yourself in a position of greater influence, you're going to have to build your network. It's also a great strategy for fighting off worry and fear.

It's waiting actively. It's action, and it requires work. As you make the calls, write the emails, and send the texts, you're moving forward. Not everyone will say yes, and some meetings won't initially lead anywhere, but the most important part is that you're moving. And honestly, that's part of the fun.

You're writing a story. Your one and only story.

You're not stuck in the worry zone. Life hasn't forgotten you. You're being prepared. There's no reason to wait around passively or recklessly. Instead, wait actively. It's why you're taking action—*this month*.

Our goal is that you'll build your network by three people over the next four weeks. That's pretty aggressive, so let's be clear what we mean by this. You're going to have the names of three people in your network who aren't currently there. This doesn't mean you've met with them yet, though that would be fantastic; it just means you are one step closer to meeting with them.

If you were to do this each month for one solid year, you would have thirty-six new names in your personal network. I guarantee you that doing this will help you discover what's next . . . and beyond.

And guess what? You now have a plan to help you get there. Here it is:

1. Make a list.
2. Make the calls.
3. Set up the meetings.
4. Ask the questions.

Finally, and this is so important, follow up with a thank-you note. Personally, I like going further than that. If the meeting is particularly helpful and they have agreed to help me by reaching out to that person they know whom I need to know, well, a carton of Jeni's Splendid Ice Creams is in their future.

A generous thank you always helps build your network. It's amazing how rarely this happens. Circling back and saying thank you to those who helped you will create a lasting memory for them. It causes them to help you even more. Even if that weren't true, we should still circle back to say thanks.

But the reality is that gratitude is a win-win.

When you thank those you know for helping you, you're building your personal network with gratitude. And while a thank-you note is something I'm sure you've already thought of, let me give you one idea that hadn't occurred to me.

It's called "plus one." And yes, it's another idea I picked

up from John Maxwell. At a three-day leadership event I attended, I heard him tell the story of a friend he'd meet for lunch who would always bring something of value—a book, an encouraging note and gift, and so forth. Every time John met with this friend, the friend was adding value to the friendship.

John calls this "plus one." Bring a book, share a gift, write a note. Never let someone bring more value to you than you are bringing to them. Imagine what life would be like if this is how we all lived our lives. "Never let a friendship get out of balance," John says. His point is that we must always seek to add value.

This is important for those of us who are struggling with the idea of asking someone for help, those who would rather give help than receive help. I get that.

By the way, do you know the hidden secret of why this is true for so many of us?

Hang with me because this may be a little offensive. It's not necessarily because we don't want to bother people. Honestly, it's pride. Yep, we're prideful. It takes humility to put ourselves in a vulnerable position and say, "I need help."

Networking requires humility. Asking "who do you know that I need to know?" declares you need help.

This is why figuring out what's next can be so daunting. It strikes at the core of hidden pride, stirring it up.

Before you send that email or make the request, pride is begging you to leave it alone. *Just settle! Embrace comfort! Stay put! But whatever you do,* don't *ask for help. We're fine!*

Say what you will, but deep down, pride is controlling the shots here. In fact, as you're reading this, pride is saying, *Oh, that's not true about me.*

Rarely, if ever, do good things happen when we listen to pride. It's why I read Ryan Holiday's book *Ego Is the Enemy* once a year.

My biggest enemy isn't the economy.

My biggest enemy isn't the ones who betrayed me.

My biggest enemy isn't the government.

My biggest enemy is the ego that lies within me.

Let's be honest. The reason you don't want to build your network isn't that you don't want to "bother" people; it's pride. Pride is your enemy, and it's standing in the way of your next.

Humble yourself. Ask for help. Then help those who help you.

If you're still struggling with this, think of it this way. What if networking is as much about you adding value as it is about receiving it? What if you were to become a "plus one" kind of friend who is also able to ask for help?

I can tell you what will happen. You'll be better off because you built your network, but the person who helped you will be better off because you are a "plus one" kind of person and friend.

But that's enough talk. It's time for action.

In his book *The Greatest Salesman in the World*, Og Mandino has included a great chapter on action. He writes, "My dreams are worthless, my plans are dust, my goals are impossible. All are of no value unless they are followed by action. I will act now."[13] *I will act now.*

It's time to build your network. Not tomorrow but today.

Or in the words of those great leadership experts, Van Halen, "Right now."[14]

Step #2: Create Optimal Options

The worst thing isn't being unsure of what's next; the worst thing is not being able to pursue what's next when it arrives. This is yet another reason the waiting room can be a blessing, not a curse. It provides time to create options for our future.

It's why waiting actively is a sign that you believe you're being prepared for something bigger, something you can't quite see or touch but are working toward by creating options for yourself.

To create optimal options is to do work now so you'll have an opportunity to choose later. Here are a few examples:

→ Get your financial house in order. (We'll discuss this in a separate chapter.)
→ Create more than one income stream.
→ Work a side-hustle.
→ Build your personal network. (Have you started on this month's goal yet?)
→ Focus on your physical and emotional health.

When you're debt-free, you have options.

When you have multiple income streams, you have options.

When you have a larger personal network, you have options.

When you are a healthier version of you, you have options.

Too often, we go looking for answers without any options. Creating options is far easier said than done. But as I've said before, we didn't sign up for easy; we signed up for worthwhile. You're digging ditches in a drought, knowing the rain will come someday.

Wendy and I found an optimal option when we discovered Mike Michalowicz's book *Profit First*. I first heard about Mike on the *Business Made Simple* podcast with Donald Miller. Mike described the reasons many businesses are unprofitable, even if the business generates a lot of revenue.

Wendy and I decided this wasn't going to be true about our business. We went to work creating optimal options by meeting with our amazing accountant, Belinda Randall, giving her Mike's book and asking her to listen to his interview on Donald's podcast.

Implementing Mike's simple system has been a massive blessing for our business, and our marriage. Structuring our cash flow within this system has greatly reduced the arguments that can happen in a marriage when you're feeling the stress of a cash-strapped business.

What Mike taught us to do was to capture the rain in the ditches we were digging. So many businesses, and especially entrepreneurs, work incredibly hard at digging ditches to capture the revenue rain, only to see it evaporate in costs.

This is the power of creating optimal options and why it's so important as you move toward what's next.

The more ditches you dig, the more rain you'll capture.

The more options you have, the better answers you'll find.

A Terrible Question to Ask

For decades now, we've been asking teens a terrible question: *What are you going to major in?* This is a terrible question because of *when* it's asked. How can they possibly know the answer? They haven't lived long enough to discover their true strengths and talents. What they're interested in is only half the battle. They need more life experience to send them on the path.

It's why I think our educational system has failed the next generation in many ways.

It's astonishing how college students can graduate and yet be financially illiterate. Not to mention, saddled with massive amounts of student loan debt.

I'm all for education. I'm not for financially strapped college graduates who will never recover from the debt, and never have options to pursue their best next.

The goal of college should be to create optimal options upon graduation. That's why, if I were the president of the Henderson University Bulldogs, the freshman year curriculum would focus on three overarching subjects: financial freedom, working internships, and discovering talents and strengths.

Freshman year at ole Henderson U. would be much more practical than what's happening at most universities. Most freshman years are simply the thirteenth year of high school, a Greek-life party accompanied by that enormously pressure-inducing question about your major.

No wonder the average college student changes their major two times, often three. The pressure of trying to figure out what to do with the rest of your life is enormous, especially at eighteen, nineteen, and twenty years of age. But here's the secret for the rest of us: we're still trying to figure that out too.

We often take on the same pressure of the "rest of your life" dilemma. As a result, our next step seems like a Rubik's Cube, with limited time to figure it out.

A better question for students would be, "Over the next couple of years, how can you discover what your major could be?"

There's a similar question for the rest of us, especially those of us in the waiting room: *In this season of waiting, how can we discover what our next step should be?*

This leads to one of the key principles in finding your best next step: *the better options you create, the better answers you'll find.*

The better options you create, the better answers you'll find.

Again, the worst thing isn't being unsure of what's next; the worst thing is when what's next arrives and you're not able to pursue it. To create optimal options is to work to give yourself the opportunity to choose.

Side-Hustles

It's why, when people ask me if they should leave their job, I ask them about their options. And yes, sometimes we find ourselves without a job. If that's the case, return to the section above about *building your network*. It's the single biggest strategy to implement when we don't have the luxury of time.

I'm a big advocate of side-hustles as one of the best ways to figure out what to do next. Working a side job when you have a full-time job is no easy task, but it does help you create optimal options by exploring rather than simply guessing.

For example, I'm often approached by people who ask if they should become a Chick-fil-A operator. My answer is, "I don't know, but I know how you can find out. Apply for a part-time job at your local Chick-fil-A."

There's nothing like real-time data to help you determine whether you love the business. If you don't like your part-time job there, you're not going to enjoy your career there. That's the beauty of a side-hustle—you get paid while exploring whether this may be your best next.

After my advisory board meeting I mentioned in chapter 1, I knew I needed to pour fuel on some current options to see if they would turn into optimal ones. I had to "pay attention to where the momentum is."

There was momentum with the *Know What You're FOR* book because it was scheduled to come out later that fall. I asked a friend who has published multiple books to have lunch with me. (See, I don't just tell you to leverage and build your network; I do it too.)

It was a lunch with Tim Irwin that changed this rookie author's life. "Books sell speeches, and speeches sell books," Tim told me. "You've got to hit the road."

Instantly, I found another side-hustle. Two actually. The first side-hustle was to pursue the idea of a business breakfast tour. Since I was a pastor, I asked my pastor friends if they would host a business breakfast tour stop as a way for their church to serve their local business community. I asked twenty-five people. All said yes.

Then I needed to figure out a way to pay for this. Enter my second side-hustle—finding a book tour sponsor. After a couple of rejections, I found a yes from Michele Velcheck and Solid Source Realty—for which I will be forever grateful.

Books sell speeches, and speeches sell books. They also create optimal options because one night on this book tour, I called Wendy and said, "I think I've found what's next."

There were other side-hustles. I launched a couple of new online courses to see if one would resonate. I worked to grow my email list. I leveraged and served my personal network, like I challenged you to do.

All of this wasn't random work. Wendy and I were creating optimal options. We knew there would always be some sort of risk in leaving, so we went to work shrinking that gap. We were digging ditches, not knowing when it would rain, but fully expecting that someday it would.

It's why side-hustles are one of the best ways to leverage the waiting room. Remember, waiting actively is the goal. You haven't been forgotten. You're being prepared for something better.

In some ways, creating optimal options is like shadowboxing. The term *shadowboxing* refers to being in the boxing ring all by yourself, throwing punches at no one. You see it either as a waste of time—after all, there's no championship belt for the shadowboxing champ—or as a training camp to prepare you for the big showdown: you versus fear and doubt.

Even if you can't articulate it completely, see it clearly, or understand it fully, you must acquire the inner belief that the best is yet to come. Better days are ahead. You're in the ring for a reason. You're in the waiting room for a season.

Do you believe that? If so, you need to answer the following question: *What optimal options am I creating financially, relationally, physically, emotionally, and spiritually?*

What optimal options am I creating
financially, relationally, physically,
emotionally, and spiritually?

Make a list and get to work. You're waiting actively.

Step #3: Find Your Muse

One of the more perplexing aspects of the waiting room is dealing with uncertainty about what we're waiting for.

Have you ever been asked, "What do you want to do?" and been frustrated because your answer is, "I'm not sure"? I get it. I've been there too.

It's why, if you don't know what to do, you need to find your who. Find someone who inspires you and follow where their path is going. Find your muse.

A muse is defined as someone who serves as an artist's inspiration. Whether you know it or not, you're an artist. You're painting on the canvas of your one and only life. Every great artist needs great inspiration. But here's the thing I've realized about inspiration. There's a difference between getting inspired and remaining inspired. Getting inspired requires a moment; remaining inspired requires a plan.

There's certainly nothing wrong with getting inspired, but it's usually like a boy band. Short-lived. Remaining inspired is the Beatles—a long, long shelf life.

> Getting inspired requires a moment; remaining inspired requires a plan.

If you're going to find what's next, you're going to need to remain inspired. And that's where a muse comes in. I'm not saying you copy them; I'm saying you *emulate* them.

Sometimes it's hard to articulate exactly what you want to do, especially if you've never done it before. There are times when you need to find a guide, someone who is where you want to be, to help provide a course to follow. In other words, find your muse. For example, I have several muses who help me remain inspired. Here are a few of them.

Shortly after I had been given the charge from my personal advisory board to start thinking about what's next, I had the opportunity to visit Michael Hyatt. He reached out to me to help coach him and his team on the training I do for public speaking.

Sidenote: It's uncanny how often this happens. When you start moving toward what's next, things start moving toward you. As a person of faith, I don't believe this is a coincidence. In any case, this meeting with Michael Hyatt happened out of the blue. He posted a question on Twitter, asking his followers who they would recommend as a speaking coach. Many people suggested me. He reached out, and a few weeks later, I found myself meeting with him at the Michael Hyatt offices.

I had been an admirer of Michael for some time. When I went to his headquarters that day in Franklin, Tennessee, I saw a picture of what I wanted someday—a thriving, passionate team that served leaders with fantastic and helpful content. And yet Michael owned the business; the business didn't own him.

He walked to work. He had a sustainable, thriving pace. He loved his work, but it didn't crowd out the most important part of his life—his relationships. He was truly living out a life principle I've tried to emulate: *our lives move to a better place when we move at a sustainable pace.*

I drove away with that picture in mind. There are times when pictures are better than words. You see it, even though you can't quite describe it. When I've had a bad day, when things don't go according to plan, that picture is still there in my mind. I walk to it. It's an anchor.

There's something about what I saw that day that draws me forward. I remember telling Wendy when I returned home from being with Michael and his team, "I don't know exactly what we're moving toward, but I think I saw it today."

Jeni Britton Bauer is another example. I've already mentioned Jeni's Splendid Ice Creams, and I'm sure I'll mention them a time or two before we're done. Observing Jeni's persistence and passion through inevitable ups and downs has helped me keep going.

An example is the day she posted the following screenshot on Instagram. She received a news alert about job openings at Goldman Sachs, and on the bottom left side, she wrote a message to her followers.

I was having a particularly hard day that day. And on those hard days, I have a tendency to think about security. It sounded like this:

→ A normal nine-to-five job would be way less stressful.

→ What if this doesn't work?

→ I wonder if so-and-so is hiring.

And then I saw this post from Jeni. It guided me back, reminding me that I was exactly where I needed to be. I was on the right path. Sure, social media has its issues, but in this case, Jeni leveraged her social media to keep me on the path.

And then there's John Maxwell. John's ability to move seamlessly through the business, church, school, government, and other fields is a path I want to follow. One of John's hopes before his life here comes to an end is to see a country transformed by values-based leadership. Those three words—*a country transformed*—kicked my butt. (As a former pastor, I can't use the other word for *butt*, even though it's in the Bible. After all, my mom is going to read this book.)

"A country transformed" is a vision worth adopting. "Needing health insurance" is massively important and needed. In America now, it's actually required by law. But ultimately, it can't be the sole determining factor when it comes to the vision for my life.

It's why John is such a helpful muse. I saw things in him that resonated with me, that drew me forward.

I'm no Michael, Jeni, or John. That's not the point. The point is that sometimes you need a picture, a persona, a muse, an image, of what you're striving for. This will look different for everyone. It should. Who might that be for you?

If you can't completely describe with words what's next, can you find a picture of someone doing what you would like to do? It doesn't have to be a perfect match, just enough for the inspiration to rise above the inevitable challenges that will try to block your way.

It's a great strategy when you're in the waiting room: *when you don't know what to do, find a who that inspires you.*

It's why the three greatest muses of my life are Wendy, Jesse, and Cole. My overarching, grandest next is to finish life exceedingly well. To do that, I've got to get better. Each day, I pray that Wendy gets a better husband today. (Not a new one! The same one, only better.) Each day, I pray that Jesse and Cole get a better dad today.

Back to my earlier point about remaining inspired, this pushes me forward. I want to finish well, and they are my muses to get there.

I want to be the best version of me I can possibly be, so I surround myself with influences, examples, and stories that will help me finish life well. That doesn't start years from now; it is implemented every day.

Again, if you don't know what to do, find a who that inspires you. Walk their path until you find your own. It's usually a blessed path to follow.

Step #4: Developing a Personal Advisory Board

One of the most helpful decisions I've ever made is developing a personal advisory board. I picked up this idea from author Jim Collins. He was being interviewed about his book *Good to Great* when I heard him say something that changed my life: "If Coca-Cola has a board of advisors, you should too."[15]

I loved this idea for two reasons. First, I'm an Atlanta native, and we're bound by law to love Coca-Cola. More importantly, it made me ask the question, "Is Coca-Cola more interested in making the right decisions with sugar water than I am with my one shot at life?"

I immediately went to work. Like many of you, I wasn't quite sure where to look, so I began to take my clues again from Coca-Cola.

> What qualifications are they looking for in board members?
> What are their decision-making criteria?
> What is their process for how long someone stays on the board?
> How do they run their meetings?

As far as I can tell, Coke doesn't publish this information, so I decided to make it up as it related to my board. Before I share this with you, though, I have to point out one of the most pivotal principles in helping us know what's next.

It comes from a passage in the Bible, and no matter

what your opinion is about that, this is a principle we can leverage or crash against: "Plans fail for lack of counsel, but with many advisers they succeed."[16]

This is one of the greatest pieces of advice you and I will ever receive when it comes to finding what's next: *the better counsel I have, the better answers I'll find.*

Once again, this is an example of waiting actively. Putting yourself on the other side of very wise people whom you would like to emulate and asking them great questions will catapult you closer to what's next. I guarantee it.

Whenever I talk about my personal advisory board, I'm often asked, "Where did you find them and what do you do in the meetings?"

The following is my approach to finding board members, determining what we talk about, and planning what a typical board meeting looks like. I'm not suggesting you follow this path exactly, but I am suggesting this is one of the best decisions you'll ever make to find what's next.

Before I go there, don't forget *why* we're doing this. We aren't meeting to meet; we're meeting to make the wisest decision possible, which is why my advisors were involved in every key decision in my life over the last fifteen years, especially when it came to finding what was next for Wendy and me.

The Who

There were three key indicators of the kind of people I wanted on my personal advisory board: (1) older, (2) wiser, and (3) experienced.

First, they weren't exceptionally older than me, though I often told them they were. While it's certainly true that we can learn a lot from young leaders, I wanted someone who had their own scars and battles, which I could leverage and learn from. Plus, I wanted their advice on marriage, finances, health, parenting, and issues far beyond work.

Second, I personally had seen the wisdom in their lives. As I often told them, "I want to grow up and be like each of you one day. I want our kids to be like yours, our marriage to be healthy like yours, our finances to follow the same principles." When we're able to glean wisdom from someone who is farther ahead of us, it's such a gift.

Finally, I wanted someone with a track record of experience. It's worth noting that none of my four board members worked in the same field, nor were they working in my career field at the time. I preferred it that way because it gave me a broader perspective.

Sidenote: I limited my board to four people. I don't have a specific reason, but three seemed too few and adding another voice seemed a bit too much for me.

The Agenda

I'd bring four basic questions to most of the meetings:

1. What am I excited about?
2. What am I worried, anxious, or angry about?
3. What one area do I need the most help with?
4. What would you do if you were me?

We'd typically follow this flow, though the board sometimes decided ahead of time what we should talk about.

We'd meet once every six weeks, though we had times when we had longer gaps and times when we met more frequently than that. Also, at least once a year, Wendy came to the meeting. I wanted the board to hear if there were any gaps in what I was telling them. I wanted them to hear how Wendy was doing, what she was thinking, and how she was processing our life and upcoming decisions.

If you're married, I can't recommend this enough. It's healthy to process what's happening in your life with folks you trust and admire. Were there times I felt like I was on the hot seat? Absolutely. Are there times the CEO at Coca-Cola will feel like they're on the hot seat in front of the board? I imagine so. But good, healthy conflict can lead to good, healthy decisions.

Let me tell you why I keep bringing up the Coca-Cola

board analogy and comparing it to my little advisory board idea. Coke doesn't have a choice. They are required to have a board. You aren't.

Most people who've asked me about developing a personal advisory board never do it. Can I push you a bit on this point? My hunch is that you won't either. I'm not trying to offend you; I'm trying to challenge you. The reason you probably won't do this isn't because you disagree with the idea; it's because it's not urgent. To paraphrase Stephen Covey's teaching about time management, "It's important, but it's not urgent."[17]

I understand. Initially, it's hard to see the value of this when the urgent cries out for attention. Every time the urgent tried to box out the importance of time with my advisory board, a voice inside me said, *Oh, so you think sugar water is more important than stewarding your one shot at life?* That inner question helped make time for the important.

It's also how I decided to leverage the fear and uncertainty that come with finding what's next. I knew I couldn't make the best decision by myself.

Ultimately, especially when it came to what's next, I wanted a green light from each of them regarding our decision to leave and pursue this new season. I don't think Wendy and I would have moved forward without that, at least not in the timeline that we did.

All that being said, the most frequent question I get when I talk about my personal advisory board is, "Where do you find these people?"

I rarely have a good answer, though I do have a principle I've heard over the years, which has proven true: *when the student is ready, the teacher will appear.* In other words, are you ready if four potential board members were to walk into your life?

Have you written a description of who and what you're looking for? (If not, borrow mine.)

When the student is ready, the teacher will appear.

Look around at the circles of influence in your life. Tell them about this idea and then ask them, "Would you consider being a board member for the next twelve months? We'll meet six times for an hour each time, and I'll pay for breakfast, lunch, or dinner."

Sure, it may take a while to get four people to agree, but don't forget, you're moving forward. You're taking action. You're surrounding yourself with wise advisors. You're waiting actively, not passively or recklessly.

And when you get a green light from wise advisors, it's one of the best ways for you to know what's next. Remember, *"plans fail for lack of counsel, but with many advisers they succeed."*

A few days before our final day at Gwinnett Church, Lauren Espy (a longtime friend and Gwinnett's program director) and the team threw a farewell party. They set up a photo booth with confetti, and my personal advisory board members were kind enough to be there—Scotland Wright and his wife, Peggy; David McDaniel; Rocky Butler; and Keith Eigel and his wife, Leigh. These folks loved and cared for us. They listened to our ups and downs, fears and frustrations, hopes and dreams. They commiserated but always challenged. They gave me a strength I couldn't have found all by myself. They reminded me that work isn't the most important part of life. They helped me stay on track. They helped me move closer to what would come next.

They look pretty happy in this picture—maybe they were celebrating not having to deal with me anymore. Sadly for them I guess, I informed them that they're stuck with me.

What you may not see in this picture, though, is the work—the work it took in the waiting room to get to this point.

What you probably don't see in this picture are the times I said to them, "How much longer is this going to take?"

What you can't see in this picture are the times they let me just talk out loud—processing, getting it all out—which in and of itself is such a gift.

I don't show you this photo to pat myself on the back. I show this to you in hopes of giving you a picture of what can happen when you wait actively. When you're waiting, *don't wish the time away; work the time away*. Implement these four steps: (1) build your network, (2) create optimal options, (3) find your muse, and (4) develop a personal advisory board.

> When you're waiting, don't wish the time away; work the time away.

Remember, you haven't been forgotten; you are being prepared. Yes, there will be days when you feel the opposite, which is why you need to surround yourself with people who will remind you of the truth. They will point you to a moment in the not-too-distant future. They'll give you confidence in yourself. Most of all, they'll steer you to a path and remind you of one of the best ways to find what's next: Just. Keep. Walking.

Keep moving forward. Keep digging ditches. Even while you wait. Especially as you wait, knowing all the while that the rain is coming.

CHAPTER 4

Finishing Well

I woke up in Florida unemployed.

It was two days after I had left Gwinnett Church and officially entered a phase that isn't talked much about in a career transition: Before *next* there is usually *leave*. And leaving creates a wide range of emotions.

Just the night before, Wendy and I were eating take-out seafood from our favorite restaurant in Santa Rosa. While praying for the meal, I just started sobbing. Let's be honest. The only acceptable emotion before eating fried shrimp is pure joy. There's no crying in baseball or over fried shrimp dinners. And yet this kind of emotion often accompanies the act of leaving.

We've all been there in some form or fashion. I'm sure you have your story of leaving a job, or a job leaving you. Even in the healthiest of transitions, leaving well can be tricky.

In a very real sense, what you do next is connected to what you do now. It's why we need to talk about finishing well. Even if that idea doesn't apply now, it will someday. You don't have to take my word for it. Meet Chuck Allen, the host of *Cool Change*, a podcast focused on career transitions and the people who make them. He has studied dozens of transitions and makes this observation: "The best change doesn't start with beginnings; the best change begins with good endings."[18]

This was the third big career move I had made in the last twenty years. Each time, I knew that the best way to get off to a great start at my next beginning was to finish well where I was. The better you finish your current season, the better you begin your next season.

The better you finish your current season, the better you begin your next season.

It's interesting how finishing well isn't discussed much. Maybe it's what they call "short-timer's syndrome," which suggests, "I only have a short time left. What does it matter how I finish?" This kind of thinking not only devalues the organization you worked for, but it devalues your personal brand as well.

How you leave says a lot more about your character than how you start. When you start, you seemingly have a lot at stake—your future. When you leave, you think your future is elsewhere. But the effects of leaving poorly tend to bleed over into your next season.

It's important to note that finishing well requires two parties—you and the organization. How you leave an organization is within your control; how the organization leaves you is outside of your control.

Decisions will be made that are outside of your control. Finish well anyway.

Decisions will be made that will hurt your feelings. Finish well anyway.

Decisions will be made that will spark your friends to come to your defense. Finish well anyway.

Take the high road. Control the controllables. Finish well. In this chapter, I want to give you five ways to do just that.

Finishing Well Starts Today

It's tempting to think that finishing well begins when you resign or when the end of a current season is a few weeks away. The reality is that every single day, we are one step closer to finishing our current assignment.

Think about it. At the end of today, you're one step closer to packing up the office, saying goodbye, changing your email address, and starting over.

If that sounds a bit depressing, it shouldn't be. In fact, your most important task as a leader is to finish well. If that sounds like I'm overstating it a bit, consider what happens when a leader finishes well:

→ The team is positioned well for life without you.
→ The organization is built around a mission, not a person.
→ The mission isn't distracted by controversy.
→ The systems you've built carry on without you.
→ Momentum is sustained.

When we see these outcomes, it's ironic that the task of finishing well isn't often talked about in leadership circles. Perhaps it's because we think of the finish line as something way off in the future. We can think about that when the time comes, right? But achieving the items on the list above takes time. It doesn't start when we put in our two-week notice. It's far deeper and more challenging than that.

Finishing well requires planning.

Finishing well requires vision.

Finishing well requires humility.

Finishing well requires character.

And finishing well starts today.

Five Strategies to Help You Finish Strong

When I announced my impending departure from Gwinnett Church, I had six weeks to finish well. I wanted to do everything I could to finish strong by setting them up for their next chapter. I followed five strategies that helped me during this season. I think they can help you as well.

1. Communicate Your Finish Plan to the Team

We've all heard of a launch plan—the strategies to launch a business, idea, or new product. I'm simply suggesting you use the same type of thinking for a launch plan for your finish plan. Again, it goes back to the principle we've already mentioned: *the better you finish your current season, the better you begin your next season.*

While it may be tempting to coast and go play golf every day after we announce our departure, that seems like a bad strategy. (Nothing against golf!) We should honor the organization and the people we've served by finishing strong.

Additionally, I think it says something about our character and emotional health if we choose not to finish strong. Both will follow us, good or bad, into our next season. An emotionally healthy person is self-aware, honors others, and completes the work assigned to them.

An emotionally healthy person is self-aware, honors others, and completes the work assigned to them.

In my effort to finish well, I gathered our Gwinnett Church leadership team a few days after I made my announcement and walked them through the work projects for my final six weeks. Here's the list:

→ Preach a three-part vision-casting series called "The Road Ahead."
→ Lead three staff meetings.
→ Host Sunday morning online gatherings.
→ Meet individually with each of our fifty-five staff members, thanking them for their contribution and asking if I could be of help to them in the future.
→ Write birthday cards to our guest services volunteers.

I wanted the team to know I was going to honor them and the mission by finishing well. I asked them if there was anything they wanted to add to the list. And I made them this pledge, which I read out loud at that meeting:

My pledge to you is to finish strong by completing the

tasks assigned to me to the best of my ability, expressing gratitude to as many people as I can while leaving as quietly as possible.

2. Create a Game Plan for Emotional Health

Emotions can run high during a season of transition. You must start now to prepare yourself to be as emotionally healthy as possible when this season inevitably arrives. We don't drift toward emotional health; we must fight for it.

My fight for emotional health is one reason I hired a transition coach to help me not only prepare for the new venture I was launching but process the emotions I'd feel along the way. (More on the transition coach a bit later.)

In many ways, my departure from Gwinnett Church was doubly hard because I loved the people, the team, and the mission. Even though Wendy and I felt this decision was the right one, we knew we'd miss the community we had helped start. When you have a sincere love for the organization, people, and mission, it's helpful to process questions like these:

→ How am I fighting for my emotional health?
→ Who really knows what's going on inside me?
→ If I were to leave my current role in the next three months, how well do I think I would finish?

The answers to these questions will help you develop your own game plan for leaving. You'll never regret fighting for your emotional health as you finish well.

3. Take the High Road

During my final six weeks at Gwinnett Church, Wendy reminded me every day before I left for work, "You'll never get these six weeks back. Take the high road and leave well."

Taking the high road simply means, "Doing to others as you would like them to do to you."

If others go low in your transition, you go high. When you look back, you'll have no regrets. Sure, people may burn bridges, but you don't have to return the favor. You can take the high road by simply remaining silent or turning the other cheek.

When you are the one who burns the bridge, the person who is most often burned is you. Don't forget, the way you leave the organization is in your control; the way the organization leaves you is in their control.

Control the controllables. Take the high road. Finish well.

4. Express Gratitude

Over the course of my last six weeks at Gwinnett Church, I wrote more than 120 thank-you notes to staff members there and at North Point Ministries. It was just a small way of saying thank you one final time, and one additional way to honor my colleagues individually. I mailed the notes on my last day, which meant everyone would get them after I had left and therefore gratitude wasn't expected. That was by intention. Remember, *gratitude is most effective when it's least expected.*

> Gratitude is most effective when it's least expected.

5. Grieve Well

Leaving shapes what's next because it shapes *you*. For this reason, I often ask people who are closing one season to go through focused self-care and introspection.

As you know by now, I didn't wake up in Florida to a normal, full-time job. The future was as uncertain as it had ever been, and yet both Wendy and I knew, somehow, someway, that we were on the right track.

Still, what do you do when you don't know what to do? The first step for Wendy and me, as odd as this may seem, was to grieve.

Usually, a certain amount of grieving needs to take place before we can launch fully into what's next. If not, it means, for whatever reason, we weren't fully engaged where we were. But if we gave our best, poured our heart into our work, and sank deep roots into the cause and relationships, there's a price we must pay.

I once invited my friend Shelley Giglio to speak to the Gwinnett Church staff. Shelley cofounded Passion City Church with her husband, Louie, and leads sixstepsrecords and the Passion Movement. After the staff meeting that day, she shared an insight and warning that I haven't forgotten.

"I've got good news and bad news, Jeff," Shelley said. "The good news is that the culture here at Gwinnett Church is like a family. The bad news is that the culture here at Gwinnett Church is like a family. If you and Wendy ever leave, it will be very painful for both of you."

Shelley wasn't saying it's better to create a stale, void-of-emotion culture. She was just looking out for us as friends, reminding Wendy and me there's always a price when we lead with the heart.

You probably didn't get this book to hear about grieving. But to step fully into what's next and to experience the full freedom of doing so, we will need to grieve what we left behind.

Unprocessed grief is a silent killer. If not dealt with, it goes underground and then appears in places, like emotions and relationships, in unhealthy ways. When we leave a job or the job leaves us, or when a relationship or season closes, there is a loss. And these losses need to be mourned.

In a post on his website, my friend Carey Nieuwhof wrote, "A mentor told me a few years ago that he's convinced that one of the silent killers in ministry for church leaders is what he calls 'ungrieved losses.'"[19] I think this is also true for life, whether we work in ministry or not.

Leaving requires loss. And if we don't grieve the loss, it will hide. But trust me, it always shows back up, knocking on the door at all the wrong times. It's why we went to Florida for a few days immediately after our last day at Gwinnett Church. Waiting there for us were our close friends Stacy and Troy Fountain. They listened, helping us process our emotions, and gave us a safe place to vent. Looking back now, we have no regrets. When you choose to process your emotions with wise, trusted friends, neither will you.

So let's make an agreement. Remember, I'm on your personal advisory board as you read. I invite you to take some time to reflect on your previous or current season. When you leave where you are now, or if you've already left, there is loss. There's the loss of identity, or at least the one associated with that role.

Perhaps you lost a good answer to the question, "What do you do for a living?" Or maybe there was a financial loss. You had to take a pay cut or went without a steady paycheck for a while.

On the other hand, maybe there was the loss of family time because you're now on the road more than ever.

There's the possible loss of relationships. It doesn't mean relationships have to end, but they do change.

There's also the loss of security. One of the surprising losses for many people on the journey to what's next is the loss of routine. We suddenly need to find a new rhythm and patterns. Establishing new patterns can make us feel vulnerable, like walking into the break room for coffee on our first day on the job. Everyone knows one another, and we feel so alone.

This is all part of the journey to what's next.

I have huge respect for you because you're on this journey and you've made it this far into the book. Most people don't have your courage. Most people stay too long. I think they realize the pain they'll have to walk through to get to what's next, and they keep that feeling at arm's length.

For those of us who didn't have a choice, who didn't leave the job or company but the job or company left us, there are even more emotions—in some cases, trauma. That word *trauma* isn't hyperbole here. Many of you have faced trauma at work and just don't know that you did.

I say all of that to say this: knowing what's next is often a complicated, emotional, grief-ridden journey. (How's that for some good news?)

But you have to talk about grief and loss, because if you don't, you'll have a rosy, unrealistic view of what's next. When you encounter the inevitable emotions and challenges, you'll think you're doing something wrong.

But you're not. You're human. You need a safe, trustworthy place to process.

As my friend Shane Benson says, "Define the moment; don't let the moment define you." Processing with a few trusted people is a great way to help us define the moment rather than letting our emotions define it for us.

It's why, shortly after leaving Gwinnett Church, I hired a transition consultant. (That's a fancy title for a therapist.) His name was Bob Lewis. Our first meeting was a video call. I began by saying, "Bob, I have four issues—three business issues and one emotional issue."

"Let's start with the emotions," Bob said. We spent the entire hour on the emotions and didn't get to the business issues until the next time we got together.

In that meeting, I shared with Bob the conflicting emotions I was experiencing. I was excited about the potential of what was next for me, but then in a split second, I'd be overcome with the emotion of leaving something I helped launch.

One day, I was alone at home. I had just received an encouraging email about a future speaking engagement. I got up, took a few steps, and just started sobbing. It was so powerful it drove me to one knee.

"Bob, am I losing my mind?" I asked when I described

that day to him. "One moment, I'm full of joy; the next moment, I'm sobbing from grief."

He smiled and said, "Jeff, the emotionally healthy person can hold joy and sorrow at the same time."

If you're going to get to what's next, you must pass through the stage of leaving. That journey will bring joy and sorrow. And when this happens, if you're holding conflicting emotions, you aren't doing anything wrong. You're simply being courageous. And human.

No Muddy Footprints

For many of us, dealing with conflicting emotions may not seem like an urgent matter. I get it. But don't forget, finishing well is your most important task because the true test of your leadership is what happens when you're no longer there. If the organization implodes after you leave, well, that says a lot. If the organization keeps right on moving, it shows you did the hard work of modeling what effective leadership is all about.

I saw this firsthand during my time at Chick-fil-A. Jimmy Collins was the president of the company at that time. He had announced his retirement a couple of years in advance, and I had a front-row seat as a staff member to watch the transition unfold.

At his last Chick-fil-A convention with all operators, spouses, and staff members, Jimmy talked about his desire to leave no muddy footprints. "My hope is that a couple of years after I'm gone," Jimmy said, "when someone calls the home office and asks for Jimmy, the receptionist will say, 'Jimmy who?' I want to leave with no muddy footprints—my tasks complete, finishing strong, and cheering you all onward."

And that's what he did.

I've made three big career moves over twenty years. Each one was exciting and nerve-racking. During each transition I tried my best to follow Jimmy's example and leave no muddy footprints. It's far easier said than done. Finishing always brings emotions to the surface, which can result in a certain level of drama. And there's always egos crying out to be noticed.

The challenging emotions that come with what's next are why I say finishing well doesn't start in the future; finishing well starts now, knowing we are one step closer than we were yesterday.

You are going to finish. Resolve to finish well.

The way you leave the organization is in your control; the way they leave you is in their control. Control the controllables. Take the high road. Finish well.

CHAPTER 5

The Path to Your Dream Job

I've lost track of the number of conversations I've had with people who are unsatisfied with their job and looking to get out. Sometimes people are fine where they are but feel like something is missing. At the end of the conversation, I tell them I have a final suggestion, and it's the very best one I can provide.

"Go back to where you work and do your very best."

Cue the puzzled look. I can almost hear what they're thinking. *Jeff, have you not been paying attention? I'm trying to leave where I am.*

I *have* been listening, and I understand. But from my experience, your day job (and those you've had in the past) provide distinct clues about your future. Here's why: *the path to your dream job often leads through your day job.*

> The path to your dream job often leads through your day job.

This is true even for those of us who don't currently have a day job. Each place we've ever been teaches us and shows us a path. In this chapter, I want to show you how.

Finding the Strongest You

One of my first "real" jobs was in the promotions department for the Atlanta Braves. As a lifelong Braves fan, it was a dream come true. (Not to mention that Hank Aaron, the home run king, worked two offices down from me.)

This was back in the old Atlanta-Fulton County Stadium days, way before Atlanta started naming ballparks after companies. (As a sidenote, we've built more stadiums than we've won championships in Atlanta. It's a tough life.)

This job with the Braves was such a great opportunity because I had a chance to do all sorts of things:

→ work with corporate sponsors
→ manage pregame and postgame promotions
→ create promotional ideas for sponsors and the Braves
→ write television and radio scripts
→ write player features for the team magazine
→ sell program ads

One night, the person who was supposed to don the costume for our mascot failed to show up. So for one game I even got to be a major league mascot! I think I lost ten pounds from heat exhaustion in the costume.

Here's why I bring this up. In that promotions job, I realized there were some things I was good at and some things I was really bad at, some tasks I enjoyed and others I didn't. For example, I discovered I had some strong creative ideas that sponsors and the Braves organization not only liked but implemented. On the other hand, I was terrible at selling program ads. Not just terrible, but Charles Barkley "turrable."

My hands would sweat while making the phone calls. I would stutter and talk too fast. I was convinced no one would buy an ad. It was an awful experience, and I felt like a failure. That is, until my dad told me that discovering what you're not good at (let's call it a weakness) is a huge win.

"You're learning," he said. "You're learning what your strengths are and what your weaknesses are. Always play to your strengths. But you can't play to your strengths until you know what they are, and where your weaknesses are."

Okay, so I'm probably not going to be a professional program ad seller. But I learned to play to my strengths.

Fast-forward many years later to when I worked in the

marketing department at Chick-fil-A. I connected again with my friend Tommy Newberry, the founder of the 1% Club. He asked me to email seven friends and ask them this question: "What do you think I'm good at?"

Despite ending in a preposition, it's a fantastic question.

The feedback gave me clues, some I saw and some I had taken for granted. That's what we do with our strengths. They come naturally to us, more so than for others. And we assume since it's easier for us, it's easier for everyone. For example, there were employees with the Braves who crushed selling program ads. And they couldn't figure out why it made my hands sweat. They were in their strengths. I was sweating.

> **The more you recognize, understand, and leverage your strengths, the better positioned you'll be to find what's next.**

Here's what I believe about you. I'll just be honest. You don't have to believe this about yourself, but let me believe this about you: I believe God created you. God's thumbprints are on you. And because I believe this about you, it leads me to a truth about you: *God's thumbprints on you are clues about his plans for you.*

Let me once again point out that this isn't a religious book. But I do believe you have been created and gifted by God. Those gifts aren't just for you; they're gifts for the world. And the more you recognize, understand, and leverage them, the better positioned you'll be to find what's next.

I discovered this one Sunday when an elderly woman confronted me at a church. At the time, I was working in marketing at a resort called Lake Lanier Islands in North Atlanta. One Friday afternoon, my dad called to tell me a pastor friend had reached out to him about a family emergency. He asked my dad if he could preach for him that Sunday. My dad wasn't available, but he suggested me as a replacement.

Now it may seem odd for a resort marketing person to be a guest preacher, but my dad and I had gone around during my high school and college years speaking to church youth groups. It's how I learned how to speak in front of groups.

Long story short, I ended up preaching that Sunday. It was a small church, and at the end of the service, the preacher typically stood at the back of the church and said goodbye to everyone. This was in the 1990s, long before preachers got feedback on their sermon via Twitter.

Everyone was kind—until she arrived. She looked relatively harmless, probably in her eighties. (I'm convinced Dana Carvey created his *Saturday Night Live* Church Lady character based on the woman standing in front of me that day.) We shook hands. She combined a smile with a frown—a hard thing to do, by the way—and said, "You're wasting your gift."

At first I thought she was complimenting me. She was telling me I had the gift of public speaking. But I quickly discovered she wasn't there to encourage me; she was there to confront.

"Young man," she said—the phrase *young man* convinced me I was in trouble—"you have a gift. From what I understand, you work at a lake somewhere. You should be speaking. If not, someday you'll have to give an account to God as to why you wasted your gift."

And then she walked off. How's that for a nice Sunday morning at church? And yet here I am, more than two decades later, remembering what she said.

A couple of years ago, *Forbes* magazine named me one of twenty speakers you shouldn't miss.[20] When I got word of that, I thought of her. I never knew her name, but I never forgot her advice. In essence what she was saying was, "Young man, pay attention to the thumbprints."

The same is true for you. Spend time being curious about your past jobs and roles. What were you good at? What are you not so good at? What's your version of selling program ads? Don't beat yourself up over your weaknesses. You win when you see them, define them, and move toward your strengths. Your past work experience leaves all sorts of clues for what's next.

My experience is that we overlook those clues. That's why I think it's true: the path to your dream job often leads through your day job.

Specifically, I want to give you a plan for how to mine the gold that is there in your current and former work life. This will be especially important for those of you who are between jobs. You may not have a current day job. That's okay. Let's talk about what you've learned from the past.

But first let's talk about what you can do today.

The Second Mile

One of the best ways to find what's next is going the second mile *now*. This simply means going above and beyond what's expected and required of you. Sounds simple. It's actually rare.

My friend Lauren Espy is an example of this. We worked together at both Buckhead Church and Gwinnett Church. Her primary job was planning the adult worship gatherings. When we moved into our first Gwinnett location, we quickly ran out of space and needed to raise money for a new building.

She went the second mile by not only proposing an

incredible fundraising strategy but also by coming up with a gratitude plan. Every time someone hit a certain percentage of what they had proposed to give, we sent them a thank-you gift. (Speaking of the second mile, I want to give a shout-out to my wife, Wendy, who oversaw the gratitude program, upstairs in our bonus room.)

Of the three fundraising campaigns I was a part of in seventeen years, this one was by far the most successful—in large part because Lauren went above and beyond what her role required. She didn't just go the first mile (her job); she went the second mile (helping the organization far beyond her specific role). She thinks like an owner. She goes the second mile.

The best way to discover the future is to work hard in the present. Going above and beyond is the best way to do that. The second mile is the path that leads to what's next.

Make a List

Write down what you think your strengths are. If you aren't sure, I highly recommend Marcus Buckingham and Donald O. Clifton's book *Now, Discover Your Strengths*.[21] Their StrengthsFinder test uncovers your top five strengths.

Will this tell you what's next? Maybe not, but it will shine a light down the path to walk.

There are many other tests you can take as well. To help you get started, I've created a five-question exercise. If it's helpful, think of yourself as You, Inc. Think about what you bring uniquely to the organizations you have served. This isn't the place to be humble; it's the place to be honest.

——— 5 Questions for You, Inc. ———

1. Which activity brings you the most energy?
   - ☐ Administrative/Support _____
   - ☐ Marketing _____
   - ☐ Innovation/Creativity _____
   - ☐ Finances _____
   - ☐ Sales _____
   - ☐ Public Speaking _____
   - ☐ Leadership _____
   - ☐ Management _____
   - ☐ Entrepreneurship _____

2. What is one area or attribute coworkers have referred to as a strength or gift of yours?

3. Who do you know with a similar strength that you could talk to or learn from? Learning from people walking a similar path is both inspiring and helpful. Write down their name and start learning how they leveraged their gifts.

4. What can you start doing to sharpen your strengths?

   Identifying your strengths isn't enough. We must start sharpening and refining them. For example, I tell communicators one of the best ways to sharpen their presentation skills is to get more reps—to speak more. I encourage them to say yes to every opportunity early on—even if it's just with a handful of people. Again, this is the advantage of a side-hustle. It helps us sharpen our strengths instead of letting them go dormant.

   What is one activity that you could start leveraging to sharpen a particular strength?

5. Looking back over your career, what work activity is easier for you than others?

   A clue here is when others point out something you do that seemingly is effortless for you but would take them much longer to do. It may be helpful to review the list in question 1. Is there an area in your career that is easier for you than others? For example, are spreadsheets a breeze? Do you find it easy to rally a team to get a project completed? These types of "easy" activities are clues. Write them down.

My point is that we often spend more time being frustrated because we don't know what's next rather than being grateful because we know God's thumbprints on our life. In fact, I know guys who spend more time picking their fantasy football team than discerning their strengths and gifts.

Let's not do that. We're better than that. You're better than that. Be curious about who you are and how you're designed. You can start the process right now by simply going through the 5 Questions for You, Inc.

If you're not going to start there, start somewhere. If you're not going to start somewhere, you forfeit the right to complain about not finding what's next.

Find a Problem to Solve

Is there something that breaks your heart? Is there a problem you constantly wish someone would solve? Do you often find yourself thinking, *Somebody should do something about that*?

Pay attention. Maybe that somebody is you.

One of the reasons I left the corporate world to become a church planter is that I was sensing how irrelevant the church had become in the minds of my friends. That bothered me to the point that I wanted to do something about it. I wanted to help change that.

I want to help organizations understand that the aim is no longer to be the best company *in* the world; it's to be the best company *for* the world. This is where purpose and profit grow together.

I've seen way too many great people work in not-so-great organizations. We can change that, and the world will get better as we do. Can you identify a problem you want to solve? Pay attention to that. It's a clue.

Ask Your Coworkers

As we've already noted, one of the best clues for discovering your next step is to ask coworkers about your strengths. While this may feel a bit uncomfortable, you don't have to ask, "What am I good at?" Try asking something like this: "In an effort to serve you and the team better, what strengths do I have that I should leverage more?"

You could also ask this question of former coworkers: "As I'm looking to figure out what's next, what strengths did you see me display when we worked together?"

All of this goes back to a foundational principle for discovering what's next in your career: *The path to your dream job often leads through your day job.*

For example, I'm probably not going to release a new music album on Spotify. There's a good chance that's not in my future because nowhere has it shown up in my past. That's not to say right turns and left turns aren't a good decision. But even in decisions that seem like a big shift, if you look closely enough, you'll find there were clues.

Donald Miller is a great example of this. Don became well-known as a memoir writer. His book *Blue Like Jazz* became a huge bestseller, which led to a fantastic writing career.

Then one day, I noticed that he had launched a business podcast called *Building a StoryBrand*.

Wait, what? That seems like a shift.

And yet the more you understood his story, his vocational career, his background, and his talents, you began to see that while, yes, it was a change, he was leaning into his gifts, strengths, passion, and talents. He was leveraging the thumbprints on his life.

The podcast is now called *Business Made Simple*, and Don has written a book by the same name, as well as launched an online platform (www.businessmadesimple.com). He is also trying to solve a problem. He's frustrated by seeing people spend tens of thousands of dollars on an MBA and not really know how to run a business after they graduate. For an annual subscription (only a few hundred dollars) to the Business Made Simple platform, he believes he can help reduce student loan debt, give people a path to their dreams, and help the middle class financially.

Come on! That's worth leaving your life as a memoirist and becoming a business owner.

This didn't happen overnight for Donald Miller. It happened over time as he leveraged his strengths, followed his passion, and investigated a solution to a problem. He found his dream job through the path of his day jobs. Just like you will.

Finally, to close out this chapter, would it be okay if I took on a mentor/pastor role for a moment?

I don't know who told you, "You won't . . ."

You won't measure up.
You won't go far.
You won't succeed.

I don't know who told you, "You don't . . ."

You don't have what it takes.
You don't have the experience.
You don't have much of a shot.

But somehow, someway, you made it to here.

To this book.
To these words.
To this moment.

It's not a coincidence. Personally, I don't believe in coincidences; I believe in callings. And I believe when we go looking for them, they come looking for us. But some evidence is required. Some work is required.

Are you going the second mile? Are you discerning and discovering your strengths? Are you asking the people who know you best where you're at your best?

When you do, it's uncanny how things start to happen. But it's not surprising. You see, whether you believe it or not, God designed you. God created you. There are thumbprints on you. And the more you know those thumbprints, the better you know those plans. God's thumbprints on you are clues about his plans for you.

Whether you believe in God isn't the point for today; the point for today is that God believes in you.

CHAPTER 6

The Money Wall

You knew that we needed to talk about money at some point, right? I hope you don't skip this chapter because this one is where most dreams go to die.

This is the wall—the unscalable wall, or so it seems. It's the wall that prevents some from even trying. It's the wall where many give up. It's the wall that tells us to sit back down.

Money, or the lack thereof, is like a bad boss, dictating how we spend our time, pushing us around, and calling all the shots. And no one likes a bad boss.

There's another number that factors in as well—our age. When people look at their financial situation and connect it to their age, the voice starts to whisper, *Just put your head down. It's too late. The wall's too high. The climb's too steep. Just get through another day.* It's why you have to be aware of the thought that may be bouncing around in your head: *It's too late.*

My friend Michele Velcheck consistently reminds the people in her life that the opposite is true. "It's not too late," she tells us. This isn't a throwaway line for her. She has lived it. She fought hard to scale the money wall and now leads her own thriving real estate company, Solid Source Realty. This idea that "it's not too late" is one of the keys to her success.

This is why the money wall is bigger than finances. Sure, our financial reality is real, but it can often mask what's really going on. We believe it's too late, so we stop fighting back and simply accept our fate. We can't risk what's next, so we back away—not just from the wall but from the possibility of more fulfilling days. This leads some people to see their work as a penalty box between weekends. It's also why Sunday night is often the most depressing night of the week. We feel the angst starting to rise around 5:00 p.m., knowing Monday's coming and the door of the penalty box is starting to open again. In the immortal words of Loverboy, the great '80s band but not-so-great life coaches, "Everybody's working for the weekend."[22]

If I've in some way just described you, I need to give you some tough but helpful advice: feel your feelings. Don't just work for the weekends. Feel the pain of the week. Feel the uncertainty. Don't drink it away. Don't binge-watch it away. Don't "social media" it away. Feel it. Feel the depression, worry, anger, rage—whatever it may be. When it comes to finding what's next, anger can be your friend if you get angry at the right thing—the thing that's holding you back.

I'm not saying get angry at a person. Get angry at the wall. Look at the money wall and direct your anger toward it. And let your anger cause you to start the climb.

"Go for It"

If you're keeping score, this chapter has two references from the 1980s: Loverboy and—here comes the next one—Rocky Balboa.

Of all the *Rocky* movies, I think *Rocky III* is my favorite. It's Rocky versus Clubber Lang, a.k.a. Mr. T. In this film, Apollo Creed, the former heavyweight champion himself, eventually becomes Rocky's trainer after Clubber knocks Rocky out in their first match.

If I keep going, I might spoil *Rocky III* for you. Then again, you've had forty years to watch this movie, so I'll keep going.

The key point of the movie is that Rocky has lost his "eye of the tiger," as Apollo calls it. And Apollo helps him find it. In fact, go ahead and YouTube their training scenes. It'll inspire you to go for a run at a beach in a tank top. (You'll see what I mean.)

In the epic rematch, Clubber Lang tells Rocky before the bout, "I'm going to mess you up." To which Rocky famously says, "Go for it!"[23]

Come on! I'm fired up already!

For many of us, the money wall is Clubber Lang. He's trying to club us into submission. "Stop dreaming, get back in line, and just work for the man."

In the words of Apollo Creed, "You gotta find your eye of the tiger."[24] You're going to have to fight, to train, to believe that the best is yet to come. You gotta scale that wall! It's not easy, but remember—we didn't sign up for easy; we signed up for worthwhile. You need to believe that if you scale the money wall, what's next is waiting for you on the other side.

And even if it isn't, good grief, you scaled the money wall. You eliminated credit card debt. You're saving more than you're spending. You have taken significant steps to becoming debt-free. You're creating cash margin for emergencies. You are consistently listening to a financial podcast to help you stay on track because it's easy to drift into old, bad habits. These are just a few of the ways you scale the money wall.

And when you do, this reality will generate so much momentum in your life that it will pour over into other areas of your life. I've seen it time and time again when people have scaled the money wall. Opportunities just seem to flow. The financial pressure isn't as intense, and their relationships improve. (One of the biggest causes of divorce is money conflicts.)

Remember when we talked about creating optimal options? When you scale the money wall and sit on top of it for a moment, you'll be able to see and consider real optimal options like never before.

Money is the ultimate optimal option, which is why I've devoted an entire chapter to it. I know I don't know your situation, but I do know people who have scaled their money wall—and it was much, much higher.

What's most important isn't your particular situation; what's most important, to borrow a phrase from my man Apollo Creed, is this: "You gotta find the eye of the tiger." You have to convert fear into anger. And convert that anger into action.

> You have to convert fear into anger. And convert that anger into action.

Training Camp

I'm not calling you to do something foolish. Hopefully by now, you've already sensed that. But you can't give up without a fight. You may need to begin a season in which you have a focused intensity to get where you need to be financially. It's going to take a while, but it won't take as long as you think.

A great way to look at this season is to think of being at a training camp. You're getting in shape. You're getting prepared. You're doing the work. You're getting ready to scale that wall. Every dollar saved, every small debt paid, every sacrifice made, is another day in camp. You're not just training for the sake of training. There's a prize you're fighting for. In this case, it's the prize of optimal options.

When you're able to take a pay cut and still pursue your dreams, you've clubbed Clubber Lang. You've won.

How long you're in training camp depends on how high your money wall is. But don't forget. There's pain on either side. You either pay now, or you pay later. You either pursue your dreams, or you quietly let them fade away.

Two Steps up the Wall

Money won't tell you what's next, but it will prepare you to find it. Creating a solid financial situation is one of the best steps to take when your path is uncertain. Money gives you the option to decide rather than watching something else decide for you.

One of the most heartbreaking realities I see is when

someone finds what's next but can't pursue it because of money. They failed to create an optimal option. This is why student loan debt is such a massive problem for so many. It promises a great future while in reality limiting it.

Before I go any further, let me give you a disclaimer. I'm no financial expert. Fortunately, many good ones are out there. From Dave Ramsey's *Financial Peace University* to Crown Financial Ministries materials to Suze Orman books and beyond, your local bookstore has fantastic resources for you to get started. However, I do want to share the first two steps that Wendy and I took to help scale our money wall:

1. We took care of Clubber Lang. During our first couple years of marriage, we participated in two financial small groups at our church. The curricula in these groups were packed with practical strategies for managing money. They helped us get on the same page financially and proved to be one of the best things we ever did. We were challenged to do those things we know we should do but can so easily talk ourselves out of doing—such as creating a will, purchasing life insurance, and developing a savings plan. Most of all, we came up with a plan *together*—for our spending, giving, and

saving. Ultimately, when it came to our finances, we resolved to earn interest and not pay interest. Not only that, we were equipped to teach a simple plan to our kids: save 10 percent; give 10 percent; live on 80 percent. This strategy is a knockout blow to Clubber Lang.

What we didn't know at the time was that it was preparing us to take a large pay cut when I left the business world for the nonprofit world. We knew this was the right career move despite the pay cut. Sure, we had to make some adjustments, but we were able to take the leap. But this didn't happen overnight. It took a while to get there. Little did we know that each day we were getting closer to what was next.

2. Find your Apollo Creed. One of the best strategies is to invite others into your journey. As I mentioned, we were involved in two small groups. Everyone in these groups wanted to scale their money wall. They inspired, encouraged, and challenged us. We did the same for them. It was as if we were in training camp together. As one couple started paying off a significant portion of their credit card debt, another would do their best to keep up. Sure, we had a guide—in this case, a financial curriculum—but

we also had each other. We had real-life examples who were scaling their own money wall. Little did we know at the time that we were all creating optimal options for our future.

Two First Steps up the Wall

1. **Pick a financial curriculum.** I recommend the video series *Financial Peace University*.
2. **Find a small group—church members, neighbors, or friends—and work through a financial curriculum together.** The accountability is huge. I've seen people eliminate thousands of dollars of credit card debt in a matter of twelve weeks as their small group cheers them on.

Wendy and I had no idea that the training camp of these two financial small groups would one day create an optimal option for us to meet you. The ability to take that pay cut led us to a world of opportunities over seventeen years, resulting in my first book, which led to my second one. But without scaling the money wall, who knows if this would have happened?

I'm not suggesting that money is the only issue, nor am I suggesting that it ultimately has to have the ultimate say over you. I am suggesting you can scale the wall by

→ choosing a financial curriculum to study and apply;

→ joining or hosting a financial small group in your home or online, using any of the great resources out there to choose from; and

→ listening to a financial podcast once a week, which will help increase your focus and intensity.

When you do this, you're going to have a great story to tell—one you can tell your kids and grandkids—about how you beat the odds, overcame the bully, and started to rise. It's one of the best lessons you'll ever teach them.

And then there will be something else. Something you didn't see. Something you didn't expect. Something that rewards your persistence, your fight, your training. On the other side of that wall will be something you didn't know was coming your way.

That's the mystery and wonder of what's next. You often can't see it until you put yourself in a *position* to see it. Choose a financial curriculum to go through. Invite friends to join you. Get started. Convert the anger into action. Find your eye of the tiger. And when you do, here's my prediction. When you convert fear into anger and then anger into action, someday you will scale the money wall. And when you do, you'll pause, sit on top of the wall, and look out toward your future.

You'll be amazed at the view. In the not-too-distant future, you'll see what's next.

CHAPTER 7

When You Don't Know What to Do

When you don't know what to do, there are three things to pay attention to: (1) calling, (2) gifting, and (3) timing. The combination of these three leads to what to do next.

I see the combination of these three all the time. For example, when I was writing this book, I had the opportunity to visit with Stephanie Stuckey. If you grew up in the South, you may recognize Stephanie's last name.

Stuckey's was a part of our family road trips. If my brothers, sister, and I behaved ourselves on the drive, a

Stuckey's pecan log roll was in our future. But let me be honest. I always behaved myself. The decision was usually made, one way or the other, by my brothers.

Stuckey's was an iconic roadside stop, with its heyday in the 1960s and '70s. If you've never experienced Stuckey's, check out the Academy Award–winning film *Green Book*, which features a roadside stop for the two characters in the movie.

As is often the case with family businesses, a company ended up buying Stuckey's, which began a long fade into obscurity. It probably would have remained that way if Stephanie hadn't received an email from one of her dad's former business partners.

"What's next for me started with a casual email exchange with one of my dad's former partners," Stephanie said.

"He asked if I wanted to buy his remaining shares of the business. I had never really thought about it, but there was something in me that knew I had to pay attention to this. I looked at the balance sheet and saw that the company had not been doing well for five years.

"The more I thought about it, the more I knew this was something I had to do—not just buy his shares, but all remaining shares, and to become the CEO.

"Suddenly I had a pivotal decision in front of me
with a lot of risk."

You've heard me refer to the mystery of what to do
next. What Stephanie is describing is what I'm talking
about. She didn't wake up one day and think, *I'm going
to buy back my family's business.* (Though if that happens
to you, it's also part of the mystery.) Stephanie was well
established in her career, having spent thirty years in environmental law, practicing sustainability in the public and
private sectors. She had also been a state legislator for four-
teen years. She wasn't necessarily looking for a new role.
In some ways, it came looking for her.

"The more I thought about it, the more I realized I
have to do this. I will always question myself if I didn't do
this. You regret the things you don't do in life. I didn't want
to regret passing up this opportunity."

Calling

What Stephanie is describing is a calling, the first circle
in our Venn diagram. We've discussed this at some length
already, but I may never be able to adequately explain it.
A calling is when your heart and soul say yes while your

A calling is when you realize that this is one of the moments you were created for.

head says, "Huh?" A calling is when you realize that this is one of the moments you were created for. You just know. And a calling usually doesn't make a lot of practical sense.

"For example," Stephanie says,

"I was never the heir apparent. I'm number four of my dad's five kids. I'm the female. I was never groomed for the role, and I think it surprised my family that I would do this. I had never really been involved in the company.

"It was also low on my radar as far as me running the company, but the company was always on my mind. It was an amazing company at its peak in the 1960s and 1970s, and I have such fond memories of stopping at the stores and traveling with my family and stopping at Stuckey's.

"On the one hand, it didn't make sense. But on the other hand, it made all the sense in the world to me."

Most callings are like that. You see things that others don't see.

"The company that bought Stuckey's from my grandfather probably thought real estate was our biggest value. I knew our biggest values were the memories and the experiences people had with the brand."

She saw something a balance sheet couldn't see. Again, that's a calling.

It's important to point out, though, that a calling isn't forever. For example, when I left Chick-fil-A, I sensed a calling to become a pastor. When I left Gwinnett Church, I sensed a calling to serve a broader collection of businesses and churches.

I'm sure Stephanie felt a calling in her work in sustainability and environmental law and at the state capitol. She now has a calling as the CEO of her family's business.

Some callings have seasons. Some are forever. To discern between the two, you can't go solely on calling; you must discern your gifting.

Gifting

Stephanie is a gifted storyteller, and LinkedIn is her blank page to tell Stuckey's comeback story. She has had a meteoric rise in followers and engagement on LinkedIn by sharing the ups and downs, wins and losses, of her next chapter as CEO of Stuckey's.

"I think the reason people are responding to what is happening is because I'm telling this story. There are people in the story, in their lives, there's grit, there's suffering, there's redemption. There's a lot here worth connecting to," she said. She's also leveraging the leadership gift she used in her previous roles in law and politics.

"I'm a big believer in StrengthsFinder," said Stephanie.

"You should do what you're really good at. If you're really bad at math but good at writing, you should write.

"The same is true with organizations. Stuckey's had a great strength. Our family loved our customers and partners. When we fell out of family hands, they sucked the soul out of the company. They didn't understand the strength of Stuckey's brand and customer experience."

A calling without gifting is like the first couple of episodes of every season of *American Idol*. Everyone thinks they have a calling to be a singer. Not everyone can sing. But I also think we sometimes downplay or disregard our gifts because we don't think we have what it takes. Stephanie could have talked herself out of buying the business because she had never been a business owner before.

As you heard her say, "I was never the heir apparent." These kinds of statements can loom large as potential excuses. And yet her unique background, gifts, and strengths allowed her to add something the company that bought Stuckey's never had—passion, energy, and life to a dormant business.

Calling asks, "Shouldn't someone do something about that?" Gifting asks, "Could that someone be me?"

Timing

Of the three, this one can be the most frustrating.

Let's not forget that Stephanie had a thirty-year career before her current role. This in no way diminishes what she was previously doing. To the contrary, it was preparing her the whole time.

Remember what we said in chapter 5. The path to your dream job often leads through your day job. The only way to create the right timing is to leverage your current time. It's fascinating to me that being the CEO never registered with Stephanie. But once it did, it happened quickly.

"The decision took a little over a month," she said. "I consulted others. I don't have a financial background, which I think was helpful because what I brought to the table was an understanding of what wasn't on the books—the value of the brand.

"I think it's important to realize important, pivotal moments like these. In some ways, I didn't go looking for this, but when I saw it, I knew it was now or never."

But what's more frustrating and disappointing is receiving a no about a possible opportunity. A friend texted me recently about being turned down as a Chick-fil-A operator. "It's a no for now," he said, "but not forever."

I think that's a line worth highlighting.

My dad told the story of being contacted by a large church in Athens, Georgia. We were living in a small town in Northeast Georgia, so Athens had all the potential of moving to the "big city."

The hiring committee came to hear my dad preach at the church where he served. They were very enthusiastic and said they'd be in touch that week. My mom and dad mentally prepared for the move, the timing, and what would be best for both churches and our family as they prepared for the call.

The call never came.

"Maybe they'll call one day. It's only been thirty years,"

my dad would say as the punch line of the story. And then he would share with us his perspective of being in his eighties and seeing how life ultimately played out.

"If we had moved to Athens, chances are your brother would have never met Amy, and you would have never met Wendy. And we wouldn't have the incredible grandkids we now have," he told me whenever I received a no on a potential opportunity.

"One of the biggest blessings I've ever received is when that church never called back."

It's important to note what my dad did next. When he eventually realized the church in Athens was never going to call back, he grieved the loss of the opportunity. He talked it over with my mom. They took a day or two to mourn what could have been, and then it was time to get back to work.

He had a job as a pastor. He needed to prepare his sermons. He needed to lead the church. He needed to serve the community. He brought his very best, and eventually a better opportunity came around . . . at the right time.

You can't control the timing, but you can control what you do during the time. It may be a no for now, but it's not forever. Keep your chin up. Unless you do that, you usually can't see what's next.

Keep your chin up. Unless you do that,
you usually can't see what's next.

Good News, Bad News

The good news is when you have all three aspects—calling, gifting, and timing—you'll discover what's next. The bad news is you don't have complete control over it. But you can cooperate in the process (see chapter 3). And yet when you don't know what to do, look for these three.

Find something that bothers you, breaks your heart, or you can't stop thinking about. Line up the opportunity to see if your gifting matches what you can uniquely bring to it. And ask, "If not now, when?"

Six months into Stephanie's role as CEO, Stuckey's was profitable for the first time in five years. "It was a small profit," Stephanie said, "but it was a big win."

The challenges ahead are big ones for Stuckey's but as a great storyteller, Stephanie knows those challenges make for great stories.

"I'm sentimental about our past, but I'm not one who lives in the past. The competitive landscape has changed since my grandfather launched the business. But what hasn't changed is the experience customers want in a roadside stop."

The world continues to change, sometimes dramatically. What hasn't changed is the pathway to figuring out what to do next—calling, gifting, and timing.

When you don't know what to do, that's what to pay attention to.

CHAPTER 8

Letting Go

When you leave, leave. Don't linger."

A few days before I left Gwinnett Church, my friend David Farmer told me this. I loved it, although I did point out to David that he has been at Chick-fil-A for thirty years and I've made three career moves during that time, so what does he know about leaving—but nevertheless . . . it still rings true. (JK, David.)

So much of walking toward what's next is letting go of the past. As Dr. Henry Cloud wrote in *Necessary Endings*, "Getting to the next level always requires ending something, leaving it behind, and moving on. Growth itself demands that we move on. Without the ability to end things, people stay stuck, never becoming who they are meant to be, never accomplishing all that their talents and abilities should afford them."[25]

To receive what's next, we need to open up our hands.

To receive what's next, we need to open up our hands. We can't receive what's next until we let go of the past.

We can't receive what's next until we let go of the past.

While all of this is true, the problem is that our emotions often have a hard time catching up with our bodies. It's easier to drive away physically than to walk away emotionally. When we leave to start a new season, our emotions usually linger, especially if we've given so much of ourselves to a previous season. This is why my transition consultant Bob Lewis repeatedly said on our calls, "Change is an event; transition is a journey."

During our calls, Bob often reminded me of the curve I was on. One of the things that confused me was why I couldn't put two good days together early on. I'd have a fantastic day, only to have my emotions grab hold of me the next day and pull me back.

Bob would air-draw a smile and say, "Jeff, you're on a journey. One day you're going to be up, and the next day you're going to slip back and be down. Eventually, we want to get so much momentum that you crest the hill. Until that time, give yourself some grace."

Giving myself some grace is something I don't do very often, which is sort of odd from a guy who preaches about grace a lot. "It's for everyone but me!" is sometimes how I live my life.

Not only would Bob air-draw a smile, but he would also refer to this diagram—one he often uses to coach people who are journeying to and through what's next. When I first saw this diagram, well, I saw me.

Individual Transition Journey
The "Feeling" Experience

Phase I: Endings   **Phase II:** Exploration   **Phase III:** New Beginnings

Denial
Anxiety
Shock
Confusion
Anger
Fear
Resignation
Sadness
Frustration
Approach-Avoidance
Confusion
Conflict
Undirected Energy
High Stress
Creativity
Acceptance of Loss
Hopeful but Skeptical
Impatience
Relief/Anxiety
Excitement
Trust
Enthusiasm

...and where are your team members?

We'd look at the diagram together, and he'd ask me, "Where are you today?"

Can I play the role of Bob in your life for a moment? As you look at the diagram, where are you today? Do you see in the diagram the smile that Bob would often air-draw in our conversations? Transitions are like riding a skateboard on a half-pipe. You go back and forth from high to low before finally reaching the end. You'll have moments when you don't have enough momentum to consistently crest to the top of phase III. And it's worth noting that the longest part of this diagram is the half-pipe where "the tornado" is.

Tornado—that's an apt description of how transitions can feel.

"People are often surprised by how emotionally challenging it can be to try to figure out what's next," Bob told me on our first call. He also made a prediction that proved to be true. "A good day will trick you into thinking you're farther along than you really are," he said. "Great transitions take a while."

I wish I could say he was wrong, but as I look back on the transitions in my career, I see that he was right. Bob usually is.

Making sure you have a *great* transition is why this chapter is an important one to understand and embrace. You need to identify, deal with, and let go of anything that may be holding you back.

It's easy to get practical with a topic like "what to do next." I hope you've already received practical help in the sections on the Career Risk Assessment, on what to do while you wait, and on how to climb the money wall, as well as in the tips found in other sections in the book. Still, your biggest issue may not be the hardware—finances, relational network, gifting, and so forth. It may be the software—our emotional awareness, our emotional intelligence, the unresolved hurt, the pain of the past, a lack of forgiveness, the things that reside outside of the résumé and deep within us. These seemingly insignificant issues have the most important impact on what comes next for each of us. I'm a huge believer in building our relational network, but if we're emotionally unhealthy, we've got some work to do. Honestly, building our relational network is easier. This chapter describes where the harder work begins.

The biggest roadblock to finding what's next isn't the economy, a lack of gifting, personal finances, or risk; the biggest roadblock to finding what's next may be you.

It was true of me as well. So we're going to let go of three primary areas, or at least we'll begin the process. We'll focus on

→ letting go of past hurts,
→ letting go of past mistakes, and
→ letting go of what others say.

You may be tempted to skip this section because, after all, what does this have to do with finding what's next? In a word? *Everything.* The most consistent part of what's next for you is *you.* That was true for me too.

155

In order to gain some momentum to crest the wall of phase III in Bob's diagram, it will always have more to do with the software—our emotional intelligence. The good news is that great resources are available for building and improving our EQ.

My goal here is to give you the "big three"—three big obstacles that can stand in the way of arriving at phase III. Remember, change is an event; transition is a journey.

You are somewhere on Bob's diagram. Letting go of past hurts, past mistakes, and what others say will help you move to the top right—to phase III, "new beginnings."

1. Letting Go of Past Hurts

I love this quote from author Lewis Smedes: "When you release the wrongdoer from the wrong, you cut a malignant tumor out of your inner life. You set a prisoner free, but you discover that the real prisoner was yourself."[26]

Chances are that someone in your most recent past hurt you. Maybe the hurt was tied directly to your career. Maybe someone betrayed you at work. Maybe you did all you could to see someone get promoted and when they had a chance to help you, they chose not to return the favor. Maybe you discovered that what someone said to you about you is far different than what they said about you to others.

It's easy to hold a grudge, to work it over in your mind, to conjure up imaginary conversations hashed out in front of a crowd as you forcefully articulate the wrong that has been done to you!

Haven't we all been there?

If not, well, congratulations, and you should get out more often.

I remember hearing a pastor say that he and his wife had never had an argument in their twenty-five-year marriage. Really? Not even over the temperature in the house? Not once? No arguments meant nothing to forgive.

Well, okay, but for the rest of us mere mortals, we have endured the pain of people hurting us. I come from a tradition that speaks favorably about forgiveness. It's rarely easy, though, but it's always worth it. With that in mind, I'd like to share another great, well-known saying: "Forgive others not because they deserve it but because you deserve peace."

Recently, I read Dr. Bruce Wilkinson's book on forgiveness called *The Freedom Factor: Finding Peace by Forgiving Others . . . and Yourself.*[27] One of the key points is that you don't just forgive people generally; you forgive what they did to you specifically. In other words, instead of saying, "I forgive Mary," you say, "I forgive Mary for . . ." and then list all the offenses Mary committed against you.

I know I won't do Wilkinson's book justice, but let me

give a brief recap of the forgiveness exercise he walks us through in the book. He instructs us to list the people we need to forgive and then rank them in order of who has hurt us the most. We start with the first person on the list. Write down every specific hurt or offense they have done to you and then scratch through each offense with forgiveness.

I did that recently, and I'll be honest, I was exhausted after the first one. Remembering, recalling, and writing down each offense is a hard thing to do. But something happened when I prayed and scratched through each offense with a red pen and wrote the word *Forgiven*. I felt freer, lighter. I think that's what Lewis Smedes was getting at—the prisoner being set free is you.

I know this may seem like an odd twist in our journey in this book. One minute we're talking about the Career Risk Assessment, and the next we're talking about forgiveness. But don't forget. From the very beginning we said that what's next for you is just as much an internal journey as it is an external one.

If you land the perfect job with bitterness still inside, it will show up. And that's not your best next step. Focusing on your emotional healing is one of the best counterintuitive decisions you'll make when it comes to your next season.

As Lysa TerKeurst wrote in her fantastic book *Forgiving What You Can't Forget*, "If healing hasn't been worked out and forgiveness hasn't been walked out, chaos is what will continue to play out . . . Emotional healing is not so much a level to reach as it is a new way of thinking you choose."[28]

The longer you hold on to the grudge, the longer the grudge holds on to you. Open your hands. Release the grudge. Let. It. Go.

The longer you hold on to the grudge, the longer the grudge holds on to you.

The best, and hardest, place to begin is to make a list of those you need to forgive. Then under each name, write down each specific offense and strike through each offense by saying out loud, "I forgive you of this."

If you need help, I highly recommend both books mentioned above. We need the best version of you in this next season, and the best version of you is one who has moved on from past hurts.

I'm not going to lie to you. This is tough internal work to do. But you owe it to yourself to be free from the grip of the grudge.

It's time to let go. It's time to forgive. You deserve to be free.

2. Letting Go of Past Mistakes

There are moments when I'll be driving in my car and out of the blue I'll remember a mistake from my past. I cringe and relive it all over again in my imagination. I have far too many mistakes in my career to list them all, so I'll choose one instead.

There was the time when I was the promotions director at Lake Lanier Islands in Atlanta, and I came up with the idea to do a fireworks show to kick off our Christmas Holiday Lights season called Magical Nights of Lights. The scene went something like this:

Opening night was ninety-nine cents night—my idea.

Each car gets in for only ninety-nine cents.

It drew a record crowd—good idea.

Traffic was at a standstill throughout the islands— still good but uh-oh.

Fireworks start—they're beautiful.

Shells from the fireworks start falling on the cars— whose idea was this?

One firework explosion starts a fire on the backside of the islands, but the fire truck can't get to it because of the standstill traffic—"Where's Henderson!"

End of scene.

That was in 1994. It comes back to haunt me even now.

I tend to remember my mistakes more than my successes. This can be a hindrance because the pain of the past can prevent me from seeing the potential of the future.

I've had to learn to convert the mistakes of the past into lessons for the future.

It's why this question has been such a great help to me when these cringeworthy moments of my past come calling: *How am I better because that happened?*

When we let go of past mistakes, we should let go of the shame. We shouldn't, however, let go of what we learned. As painful as the opening night fireworks show was, we ended up having our best attendance season that year. That first night gave us a huge push forward. I personally experienced the value of getting off to a strong start.

Eventually, I found myself working at Chick-fil-A, where one of my roles was to open up new restaurants. The way we articulated the power of grand openings was through this principle: *higher initial sales equal higher sustained sales.*

Sure, mo' customers, mo' problems. I'll take those problems any day compared to a grand opening where you throw a party and no one shows up. Little did I know as I watched fireworks shells rain down from the sky on cars (yes, it still makes me cringe), that it would make me a better marketer at Chick-fil-A. You see, the year before the fireworks idea, I had experienced an opening night where hardly anyone showed up. That was far more painful. If you have to choose between a small crowd on opening night or a large crowd, I will choose the latter. As I served operators in creating their grand opening plan, I presented the contrast of those two opening nights. Sure, both have their challenges, but higher initial sales equal higher sustained sales.

Fast-forward years later to the Sunday we started Gwinnett Church. Thousands of people showed up—so many people that the police closed the road outside the church for a few minutes. Our staff expressed concern about it. I smiled and said, "Well, at least there aren't any fireworks."

I'm reminded of what the late author and philosopher Dallas Willard said to preachers: "At some point you have to release your words."[29]

Learn from your mistakes, yes. But at some point, you have to let go. If not, you'll get stuck in the past, and what's next is rarely found there.

3. Letting Go of What Others Say

I'll go ahead and say right up front that I'm not where I need to be when it comes to letting go of what others say. I discovered why during a Zoom call with my counselor—no, not Bob, my other one, Joy.

"Jeff," Joy said, "I think you might be a compulsive affirmationist."

Affirmationist? What is that? Spell-check hasn't even heard of that. I came to find out that Joy just made up the term. Maybe my claim to fame is that I was the originator of a personality disorder.

After a few blank stares on Zoom, I mustered up the courage to ask, "What is a compulsive affirmationist?"

"No matter how much affirmation you receive," she said, "it's never enough. I think when your dad passed away, this kicked in. You're missing his voice."

Welcome to my counseling sessions with Joy. Hurtful and helpful, all at the same time.

During that season of figuring out what was next, I often found myself wondering what people were thinking. *Am I promoting my business too much?* I would ask myself. *Is it okay for me to post about this or that? What if someone's not happy about what I'm doing?*

I eventually began calling my friend Troy Fountain when those thoughts came up. He was quick to remind me, "Jeff, no one's talking about you today. And even if they are, the time will be quick. They've got other things going on that are far more important than thinking and talking about you."

Tough love, but true.

And that tough love helped me to keep moving forward. I can't let *imaginary* voices keep me from what I feel like I'm called to do in this next season. I put imaginary in italics because that's what they often are.

One of the best ways to begin letting go of what others say is to make a short list of the voices that matter the most to you. For me, this obviously starts with Wendy, my kids Jesse and Cole, and then a short list of eight names.

I determined that if these eleven people were proud of me and supportive of what I was doing and where I was going, then I had to release what others may say. As I often tell communicators about whom to listen to regarding feedback, "You don't need to listen to everyone. You do need to listen to someone. Who is that?"

And even if Troy is wrong, even if people *are* talking about you, if they're not on your most important voices list, have the maturity to let go of the words they'll say.

One of the most freeing decisions you can make is to let people be wrong about you. You don't have to defend yourself, even though it may feel good. For every moment you defend yourself against what others may say, that's one more moment you rob yourself of pursuing what's next.

I'm not suggesting it's easy. Don't forget, I'm apparently the originator of the compulsive affirmationist disorder. If I pay too much attention to what others say, though, I won't be able to see what's next. Neither will you.

One of the most free-ing decisions you can make is to let people be wrong about you.

The challenge is that we will misdiagnose the problem. What we think is holding us back isn't really what's holding us back. What is holding us back is something we've never let go.

Maybe you've never let go of a past hurt; it's time to forgive. Maybe you've never let go of a past mistake; it's time to forgive yourself. Maybe you haven't let go of the fear of what others might say; it's time to listen to the right people—those who love you the most.

Letting go is often the best way to move on. To paraphrase a line from Bob, "Letting go is an event; moving on is a process."

Whenever I've forgiven someone and the thought of what they did pops into my mind, I remind myself, *I let go of that in the past. It's now time to move on.*

Whenever I'm reminded of my Christmas fireworks show fiasco and other "turrable" ideas, I remind myself, *I let go of that in the past. It's time to move on.*

Whenever the fear of wondering what people may or may not be saying pulls up alongside me, I remind myself, *I*

*let go of what others think, with the exception of my top eleven.
It's time to move on.*

Letting go is just as important as working through the Career Risk Assessment. Correction. It's *more* important. If you want to move on to what's next, you must move on from the past.

When the Dream Dies

O pening an independent bookstore in the world of Amazon doesn't seem to make much sense, unless you know it's exactly what's next for you. That's where Stacy and Troy Fountain found themselves as the owners of Downtown Books in Dothan, Alabama.

Wendy and I have known Stacy and Troy for almost twenty years. Other than being rabid Alabama Crimson Tide fans, they are amazing people and two of our very best friends.

When Stacy and Troy told me about the idea of opening Downtown Books, Wendy and I were thrilled. In a world of online shopping, I'm a big fan of in-person bookstores. But I also knew what was ahead—eventually, inevitably the dream will die. The moments of "this is harder than we thought" and "should we be doing this?" always walk across the stage of our lives.

But here's the secret for when your dream or idea dies: it can come back to life. It's all part of the life cycle of an idea. If you've never had a dream or idea die, you're not trying hard enough. It happens, especially when you're doing something you've never done before—like opening an independent bookstore.

I have this strange expectation of myself when I do something for the first time. I expect it to be flawless, as if I've done it a million times. But it never works out that way, and I'm not alone.

For example, I enjoy asking communicators about the first time they gave a talk in front of people. These are top-of-the-line communicators, and every one of them cringes when I ask this. No one has ever said, "Oh, my first talk? I *crushed* it!"

As boxer Mike Tyson famously said, "Everyone has a plan until they get punched in the mouth."[30] It's fun to dream about what's next, but when you get to work pursuing it, at some point, you'll get punched in the mouth. This chapter is about punching back. To help you do that, I'll share one of the most helpful concepts I've ever discovered called "the life cycle of an idea"—or at least that's what I call it.

I've shared this with down-and-out entrepreneurs and seen them perk up. I've shown it to discouraged communicators and watched them pick themselves back up. I've explained it to business and nonprofit leaders and heard them say, "I wish I had heard this years ago."

If you need to find some persistence, the life cycle of an idea will do that for you. It will also give you much needed encouragement and clarity.

Sometimes it's as much about knowing where you are on the journey as it is about where the journey is going. That's the power of knowing the life cycle of an idea. It shows you where you are and what to do when what's next starts to fade on you.

The Next Idea

What to do next arrives in lots of forms. Sometimes it arrives in a conversation, a text, or a phone call. And then there are those times when what's next won't leave you alone.

"This idea of owning a bookstore had been something I had thought about for years," Stacy said. "My regret over not pursuing this was starting to outweigh my doubts."

That's a great point. It's also helpful to realize the fallacy of "the timing has to be right." There's a difference between the timing being right and the right timing. When we want the timing to be right, we're usually listening to our excuses. When we look for the right timing, we look for ways to overcome those excuses.

If you're waiting on the timing to be right for opening an independent downtown bookstore in an online world, you'll never stop waiting. If you look for the right timing, you'll eventually launch. And when you do, the journey will look like this:

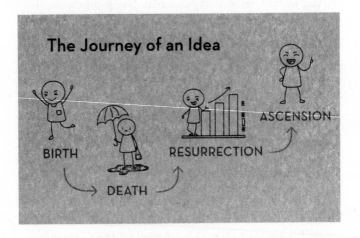

The Journey of an Idea

BIRTH

DEATH

RESURRECTION

ASCENSION

I began noticing this cycle in two areas of my life. First, I was fortunate to be a part of three new church plants, and in each case the life cycle of those three churches followed this journey. Second, I also began to notice this cycle as I prepared for a presentation I was about to give. Almost always, these new ideas followed a pattern:

→ the birth of the idea
→ the death of the idea
→ the resurrection of the idea
→ the ascension of the idea

It's very rare, when working on a talk, to not pass through stage 2. I look at my notes and think, *This is awful. I need to find another line of work.* But if I keep working through it, I'll eventually get to stage 3. The talk comes back to life and gets better for having pushed through the "death." This is true when launching pretty much anything.

Bringing an idea to life—from nothing to something—requires enormous energy and effort. And once you get to a point where you think you're almost there, somehow, someway, the idea seems to die. It's never, ever fun, but when you know this, when you know where you are on the journey, you realize you're not at the conclusion; you're just at stage 2.

This happened to me as I worked on this book. I received an encouraging text from a reader about my first book and then started thinking about this one. The fear started to rise. What if this book isn't as good as the first one? Then it just spiraled. I wanted to quit, call my editor, and say, "I'm sorry. It's just not working." I had officially arrived at stage 2—the death of the idea. Before I knew

171

how this process worked, I would have spiraled even more. Now that I'm aware of this cycle and have been through it numerous times, I know what to do. (And the good news is that you're about to as well.)

Let me explain by talking about one of my favorite podcasts, *How I Built This* with Guy Raz. It's about entrepreneurs, dreamers, and launchers who pursue a dream. Every time I listen to a new episode, I put it through this filter: There was the day or time they came up with the idea. Then there was the moment it died. Heartache, pain, loss. Or it was just harder than they expected. (Sidenote: it always is.) And then, through their persistence, the idea resurrected; it came back to life. And then, based on what they now know, the idea ascended into something even greater than they expected.

This is what happens as I listen to every episode of *How I Built This*. Let's use the story of Jeni, the founder of Jeni's Splendid Ice Creams.[31]

→ **The birth of the idea:** Jeni opens her first ice cream shop called Scream. (By the way, I love that name for an ice cream shop.) Scream gains some early traction and fans. Jeni is experimenting with all sorts of different flavors but doesn't keep some flavors in stock. Eventually, Scream dies.

→ **The death of the idea:** Scream closes. End of story. This is where most stories stop. And maybe this is where you find yourself. Your idea of what was next got too hard. It didn't work out. It failed.

→ **The resurrection of the idea:** One day, Jeni visits her favorite coffee shop and orders her usual orange scone, only to be told they're all out of orange scones. Jeni slowly backs out of the restaurant, realizing that this was part of her story at Scream. She was coming up with new recipes constantly, which meant there was no consistency. Customers ordered their favorite ice cream, only to be told that their desired flavor wasn't available that day. *Maybe that's one of the reasons Scream didn't work,* she thought. This sparks her interest in rethinking everything about Scream, and eventually it leads to Jeni's Splendid Ice Creams.

→ **The ascension of the idea:** The idea of one ice cream shop has now ascended way beyond Scream to a multimillion-dollar business in forty-seven locations and nationwide distribution.

Jeni isn't the only one who has a story like this. But don't take my word for it. You should listen to other episodes of the podcast and find out for yourself. Story after story is about the life cycle of someone's idea. They were pursuing what was next, and then the dream died—but then you hear the rest of the story.

I found myself in stage 2 that day while writing this book. I needed to be reminded that I had been here before. I needed to hear a story or two to remind me, so I went for a walk and listened to an episode of *How I Built This*. I knew what I needed to do—go get some perspective and, eventually, keep writing.

Now let's talk about you.

Where are you on this life cycle as it relates to what's next? It may be finding a job, finding a spouse, finding a new workout plan—anything that's a best next step. Maybe you've been thinking about starting that business, writing that book, applying to that school. The birth of the idea is the fun part. I'm fascinated about the idea process—whether it's a business, a song, a book, or whatever it may be. I love asking people, "How did you come up with that idea?" A billion businesses have been launched in the minds of people. That's fun, exciting, and intriguing.

But there's a danger. The birth of the idea is where many live and never leave. The idea simply remains in the mind. Everyone can have an idea in the shower. The difference makers towel off and go do something about it.

It's easy to say, "Someday I'll open up a bookstore." It's

something entirely different when you sign the papers to lease the space.

If you've been thinking of an idea for more than a year and haven't taken a step toward it, you should do yourself and the people in your life a favor. Stop talking about it. (Get ready for some tough love coming your way.) The reality is that your idea is all talk. You've researched it for hours online. You've talked to plenty of people about it. But you haven't taken action. Real action.

I've spoken to plenty of people who have told me they want to write a book someday. They have an intriguing idea for a novel or want to write a book on leadership or a book for children—and the list goes on and on.

I love hearing these stories, but then I ask the hard question: "How many words have you written?" That's usually when the conversation gets awkward. It's better to do the work and not talk about the idea than to talk about the idea and not do the work. (Okay, tough love speech over.)

It's better to do the work and not talk about the idea than to talk about the idea and not do the work.

Don't forget. Bringing an idea to life—from nothing to something—is a massive accomplishment requiring tons of energy and discipline. And if that wasn't hard enough, you eventually find yourself ushered into stage 2: the death of the idea.

Granted, death sounds a bit dramatic. Sometimes it's not death; it's just a massive roadblock. And yet there *are* times when the idea dies. And it feels like a death.

The third and final church I helped launch was in a former Winn-Dixie grocery store. Ironically, Buckhead Church, the first church I led, also started out in a former grocery store. I felt like I had come full circle.

When we launched Gwinnett Church in 2011, I proposed that we name the church after the county because I was convinced we needed to have more than one location in Gwinnett. Eight years later, an opportunity arose to do just that in a town called Hamilton Mill.

When I drove to the site for an initial visit with our team, I instantly knew this was what we should do. I told my friend Al Causey in the parking lot, "I don't even have to go inside. We should do this." That's the birth of the idea.

We did end up going inside, walking around and dreaming together, and gathered at what used to be the former checkout lanes of the Winn-Dixie. We went around the circle and did what we call "fist to five." If you disagree with the decision, it's a fist. If you agree with the decision, you hold up all five fingers. If you're somewhere in the middle, you hold up a few fingers. If you're really opposed, I guess, you hold up your middle finger.

Every single one of us held up all ten fingers. We were doubly all in! Our second location was about to be born! The very next day, a company presented a contract to buy the building out from under us. The idea died.

When I got word, I was more than disappointed. I was a bit confused. It seemed cruel for us to get excited, only to have the rug pulled out from under us. Fortunately, I knew two things were true. First, as my father-in-law, Everett Major, says, "It's not a done deal until someone has a check in their hands." This was far from being a done deal. This idea was dead, but it wasn't buried.

Second, I knew we had simply arrived at stage 2. This didn't mean we would automatically get the building. I believed if this former Winn-Dixie grocery store wasn't our best option, there would be a better one in the near future. (Sometimes an idea dies so that a better one can find the light of day. Case in point: Scream Ice Cream.) The key is understanding how to get from stage 2 to stage 3, knowing how to bring the idea back to life, seeing it transform into something else.

For example, Slack, the employee communication tool, actually started out as a gaming company called Tiny Speck. The founder, Stewart Butterfield, and his team built a communication tool for themselves, never intending it to become their future. In fact, if Tiny Speck had not died, there would be no Slack. The death of the idea introduced them to their billion-dollar future.[32]

The point isn't to keep pushing the initial idea beyond good wisdom. The point is to keep pushing. As you do, you've got to figure out where to push.

I wasn't giving up on the Hamilton Mill location until somebody had a check in their hands. I talked about it as if it were going to happen. I thought about how our staff should be structured. It was a much smaller location, but I began to talk about a new trend I was seeing: "Small is the new big."

Yes, the idea had died, but until it was buried, I was going to do my best to bring it back to life. And that's the ultimate question when it comes to the life cycle of an idea: How do you keep moving so that you get to stage 3?

I'm so glad you asked. I have two thoughts that have been extremely helpful for me.

1. Don't Ask, "Is This Working?" Ask, "What Am I Learning?"

David Butler is the chief growth officer of Kids2. Before that, he led innovation initiatives at a little soft drink company you may have heard of called Coca-Cola. David and his team created one of my all-time favorite products—the Coca-Cola freestyle machine.

It's soft drink heaven, truly brilliant.

Imagine David's role. He was the one responsible for new products and innovation. It's why I asked him, "As a publicly traded company with so much scrutiny, how many failures do you get before the next product has to work?" David's answer has helped me move from stage 2 to 3 over and over again. "I can't look at it as a pass/fail," he said. "I can't ask, 'Is it working?' I have to ask, 'What are we learning?'"

This is in essence what happened with Scream Ice Cream and Tiny Speck. The day without the orange scone led Jeni Britton Bauer in many ways to that question. What could she learn from the experience with Scream Ice Cream that she could apply to her next idea? The very same thing happened at Slack. "Wait a minute! Maybe this tool we created to help our team communicate is the idea we should pursue!"

From death to life. It all comes down to being more curious, to letting the failure teach and guide you.

If you consider your last season a failure, or if what you started didn't work, there's gold in the hills of that failure if you'll take time to think and mine for it. Most people I've spoken with beat themselves up over their failures rather than taking the time to write down the lessons they learned in the process. The seeds of your best next step are usually found there.

2. Failure Is an Event, Not a Person

Don't get the definition of failure mixed up. If you do, you'll decide you're a failure and won't push through to stage 3.

For the last twenty years, I've coached communicators on how to make their next presentation their best presentation. A key differentiator between communicators who thrive and those who don't is their ability in the early stages of the talk's development to see feedback as helpful, not personal. In other words, they can separate themselves from the presentation and not view criticism as a personal attack. The presentation may fail, but that doesn't mean *they* are a failure. They understand failure is an event, not a person. The communicators who can get to that point are the ones who will soar.

Can I ask you a personal question? If you're coming off a rough season where something didn't work, have you concluded that you're the failure? Can you see the situation as an opportunity to learn? And can you take those lessons and let it impact what's next for you?

It's taken me years to get to this point, but I've started to stand alongside my failures instead of seeing them as within me. These failures are events; they aren't me. To borrow a phrase from Donald Miller, I'm "a hero on a mission."[33] Heroes have plenty of failures, but eventually they rise. Heroes don't stay down.

And since you're a hero, you have a choice. You can let stage 2 be the concluding chapter, or you can let stage 2 be a chapter in an even greater story. Here's what I also love about the stories I hear on Guy Raz's *How I Built This*. The stage 2 chapters make their stories even better, grander, and more robust.

Imagine if Jeni had opened Scream and it took off. That's a great story, but I'm not sure the company would be as great without the challenges. Or think about if Stewart Butterfield had launched Slack without any problems. The product wouldn't be as good without the tweaks and improvements. But we can't have any of that without stage 2.

Best of all, our challenges mark us for the better. They put dents in our egos that are buffed out with stronger character. They create wrinkles in our foreheads that lead to strength in our minds. Stage 2 makes us who we are. It forces us to grow, to stretch and fight, to fill a larger space.

Think of your situation and story this way: If you were a scriptwriter writing the movie about your life, how would you write the next chapter? What would you do next? Can you separate what happened from the person it happened to?

This is the pathway to bring back to life your idea for what's next.

I love watching Troy and Stacy fight to bring a bookstore to life. They faced crazy challenges, like not being able to find bookshelves due to supply chain issues and trying to master all the intricacies of building codes, learning the sales tax policies, and hiring a team during a labor shortage—once they solved one issue, three others popped up. By the way, do you know how many times people have reminded them that Amazon sells books online nowadays and that people don't go to in-person bookstores anymore? (One thing life isn't short on is the naysayers.)

"For me, the biggest roadblocks have been internal," Stacy said. "I find myself thinking, *Can we do this? We don't know what we're doing. After all, we've never done this before!* Then I'll think, *No one buys books anymore,* which isn't true, but your mind tries to convince you to buy into the lies and doubts. The obstacles, setbacks, fear, and failures, if you want to call it that—it's all part of the story."

As writer Ryan Holiday reminds us, "The obstacle is the way."[34] In other words, every great story requires a villain. There can't be a great story without villains such as challenges, defeats, and obstacles to overcome. As much as we dislike the villains, we need them so we can write a better story with our lives.

Batman needs Joker.

Coke needs Pepsi.

College football needs Nick Saban.

Every hero has a villain. Every hero has a dark night of the soul. Every hero has a great cause. You are not the failure. You are on a journey. Your "villain" may be the way to find what's next.

And if you find yourself in stage 2 of what's next, guess what has happened to you—the journey has led you to this chapter. Maybe this chapter is the very reason you're reading this book. It's part of the mystery of finding what's next.

Your idea for what's next is inside you, whispering, *This is just part of the story. Keep going.* Just. Keep. Walking. You never know what you'll discover if you keep walking, convinced that the idea, in some form or fashion, will be resurrected.

On the day of the closing of the old Winn-Dixie building, I woke up knowing one way or another the story was going to become even more interesting. As you'll recall, a company had offered to buy the building the day after our initial tour, and now the day had come for them to put a check in someone's hands.

Honestly, I wasn't surprised when I received a call from Rick Holliday, the chief financial officer of North Point Ministries. "Jeff, you may not believe this," Rick said, "but the deal fell through today. We've got another shot to buy the building."

A year later, we officially opened Gwinnett Church Hamilton Mill. That opening Sunday was one of my all-time favorites for so many reasons. It reminded me that greater stories come with greater conflict. Very few people in the building that day understood how unlikely it was that we were all standing there. It was a journey made even better because the idea had died.

If your idea is on life support or has faded away, I think it would be helpful to review the "Journey of an Idea" illustration. In fact, text me at (404) 317-3946, and I'll send it to you. It will help remind you that each idea, each next step, is a journey. Keep moving forward.

And as your self-appointed personal advisory board member, please allow me to speak some truth over you today with this recap:

Failure is an event, not a person.

You are a hero on a mission.

Don't ask, "Is it working?" Ask, "What am I learning?"

Your idea for what to do next is somewhere in these stages:

→ the birth of the idea
→ the death of the idea

→ the resurrection of the idea
→ the ascension of the idea

Oh, and one final suggestion. It's amazing how quickly I can forget how hard it is to bring something out of nothing. And it's easy to fall prey to thinking I should be great at something I've never done before.

It's why I have a fun idea to help you remember that you need to keep walking, to move from stage 2 to stage 3. Not only will it help spur your dreams, but it will also help encourage two wonderful people to keep pursuing theirs. So if you ever find yourself in Dothan, Alabama, stop by Downtown Books and ask for Troy and Stacy. Ask for this book, and they'll give you a signed copy. Chances are, though, you won't find yourself in Dothan anytime soon. So score one for the little folks in the independent bookstore world by buying another copy of this book at Downtownbooksdothan.com.

When your book arrives, put it where you can see it frequently, especially when your idea, speech, or new business seems to have hit stage 2. The book will remind you of the life cycle of an idea and that your current obstacle isn't the conclusion of the story; it's just a chapter.

It will also remind you there are still dreamers and doers in this world. And you're one of them.

CHAPTER 10

What Next Feels Like

I was on a walk one day, and I came across this guy.

"Buddy," I said out loud, "I know how you feel."

During one particularly challenging season of figuring out what's next, I felt splayed out on my back with no hope of getting up. I shouldn't have been surprised. The Shirelles have been singing about this since 1961: "Mama said there'll be days like this."[35]

Days like this happen often on the climb to higher ground. You're reaching up for higher ground, only to lose your balance and topple over. It reminds me of the movie *Free Solo*—you know, the one where that guy climbs the three-thousand-foot rock face of El Capitan . . . without a rope. Never have I palm-sweated more in a movie than that one.

That guy is Alex Honnold, and he won an Academy Award for the documentary about the climb.

I'm also reminded of the gritty Batman film *The Dark Knight Rises* when a fellow captive advises Bruce Wayne to make the climb out of the pit they're in "without the rope."[36]

The Dark Knight is fiction. Alex is real, and so is El Capitan. All three thousand feet of it. And that mountain you're trying to climb? It's real too.

My hunch is that's what happened to my friend the turtle. He tried to climb the mountain—from my perspective a small embankment, but to him a mountain—only to fall backward. Like you, he had an idea. He tried to climb to higher heights. Something in him said there was something just over the edge that was better than where he was. He believed there was more for him. He took a risk, only to soon discover, sadly, that he was in dire straits.

He climbed "without the rope." And when we fall, something deep inside whispers, *I told you we should have stayed where we were.* What's familiar feels like a warm blanket and a wonderful memory, especially when we've fallen backward for the whole world to see.

This feeling, this longing for the familiar, is what your

brain is searching for. It convinces you to look and stay with the same consistent patterns. They are evidence you know what you're doing. Everything is under control. We're all safe. Stay under the blanket (or inside your shell). It's cold out there.

Rope? You don't need a rope. Just stay where you are, safe and on the ground.

Our brains are important, to be sure, but if we're not careful, the fear, self-protection, and worry (all from our brains) can lull us into a false sense of safety. Our brains are searching for the familiar.

Ironically, what's most familiar can be most dangerous. The familiar can draw a blanket over our eyes, causing us to no longer see our possibilities, and that's a dangerous place to be. Sure, what's next doesn't feel comfortable, but it's not the scariest place to be; the scariest place to be is the same place as last year. No growth, no challenges. Just the same.

The scariest place to be is the same place as last year. No growth, no challenges. Just the same.

My friend David Farmer, who leads the restaurant experience team for Chick-fil-A, says, "If you're the same person you were ninety days ago, you're falling behind." That's aggressive, but then again, if you knew David, you would see how he lives this out. David is consistent at working, tweaking, and evaluating his life plan, which includes measurable goals for every area in his life. He's committed to making changes and not falling behind in life.

I'm not suggesting that you make random changes, but I am suggesting that you will always need to keep growing. If you're the same you next year, you are losing ground. Or as David says, the same you ninety days from now is falling behind.

To get there, we need a strategy against our natural tendency to play it safe and look for comfort. It's why we have to create a converter within us. We must convert these natural, protective feelings into different thought patterns.

Think of it this way. Your brain is like a hill. When rain comes down, the water forms patterns and creates ruts on the hill. Every time it rains, the water flows down these already existing patterns. The same is true when it comes to your brain. When your brain faces new problems, it searches for familiar patterns. Over time, if you're not careful, those patterns become ruts and you get stuck. If you're going to pursue what's next, you must think differently. And if you're going to think differently, you need to create new patterns of thinking.

Let's go back to the hill. If you want to change how the rain flows down the hill, you need to create a different route for the rain to follow. You can put a rock or a bale of hay on the hill that will force the water to follow a different pattern the next time it rains, thus avoiding the familiar rut. Your brain is the same. Unless you change your thinking, you'll naturally drift back to old ways, old emotions, and old patterns.

Your brain and mine are searching for safety and protection—two things that what's next rarely offers. We must convert that natural tendency into a new way of thinking.

During one season of transition, I had to convert four primary thoughts into new, positive patterns. With every fear, worry, anxiety, or insecurity, I had to convert those thoughts in order to have the courage to keep moving. This is how I created a thought converter in my mind.

Simply recognizing how my brain had been trying to keep me in safe, familiar patterns was helpful, but it wasn't enough. Once I recognized these patterns, I created a converter thought or question to move me forward. I ended up with four specific converter thoughts or questions.

Maybe you won't resonate with all four, but my hunch is that at least one of these will show up as a thought pattern that's trying to sway you toward the familiar. While the familiar isn't always bad, it rarely leads to higher ground. Converting these four thought patterns has helped me on the climb, which so often feels like one "without the rope."

1. What If This Doesn't Work?

This one was my biggest bully shortly after leaving Gwinnett Church. It also convinced me that everyone was watching to see if what I was doing was working. It's why, as I've already mentioned, my friend Troy Fountain would call and remind me, "Jeff, no one's talking about you. Don't make decisions thinking that they are."

The key to rising up and punching back was converting the question. Instead of asking, *What if this doesn't work?* I converted it to, *What if this does work?* This conversion helped me view my situation through a different emotional filter.

I started thinking more about what my life would be like if this *did* work. I saw a vision of being able to influence and help a wider group of people than just my local community. I began to see what was at stake if I didn't climb that hill.

It also helped me embrace new thought patterns and the inevitable ups and downs, knowing it's what happens when we try to climb to higher ground.

Converting *What if this doesn't work?* to *What if this does work?* may be all you need to give you the push out the door. One question gives you a false sense of safety; the other gives you a new perspective for what's next.

2. What If My Best Days Are behind Me?

In other words, what if I've peaked?

I love watching people reinvent themselves—starting a new career, blazing a new trail, even if their past one has been glorious. It's what we've already seen in Stephanie Stuckey's story. She's reinventing herself because she knows her best days are ahead. We also saw it in the story of Donald Miller, who moved from memoirist to business owner.

I'm drawn to these reinvention stories. When I see them, I know I've found a courageous person who has converted this question. Instead of thinking, *What if my best days are behind me?* they think, *What if my best days are ahead of me?*

I've already mentioned my friend David Salyers, whom I worked for at Chick-fil-A. He had a brilliant career there but decided a few years ago that the season there had come to an end. I spoke at David's retirement party, where he made his intentions clear to everyone that day. "I'm not retiring," he said. "I'm rewiring."

David is now the co-owner of a thriving coworking space in Atlanta called Roam. He's a popular speaker who teaches organizations how to create a great culture, using principles from a book he cowrote with Randy Ross called *Remarkable!*[37] He's on the board of not one but two banks. He's an investor in several start-ups, and every time I'm with him, he seems to be pursuing a new one.

What David has shown me is that Chick-fil-A was a part of his story. It was a great chapter. But there's more to the story. He didn't leave his best days behind. His best days are ahead of him.

Reinventions like this look easy, but they are far from it. In fact, it's harder the older you get. There's more at risk. You're putting your reputation on the line.

It's easier to stay put than keep moving forward. But that's why many of us get stuck. I'm not suggesting that staying where you are is a bad decision. I am suggesting if you're staying because you're convinced your best days are behind you, well, yes, that's a bad decision.

And it's how we get old in our thinking. As my friend Daniel Harkavy told me, "The older people get, the less risks they take. This is how we get old in our thinking, when in fact the opposite should be true," he said. "The older we get, the more risks we should take."

There's the story of when actor/director Clint

Eastwood, at age eighty-eight, was playing golf with country singer Toby Keith. Eastwood was starting a new movie the next day, which prompted Keith to ask, "What keeps you going?"

Eastwood replied, "I get up every day and don't let the old man in."[38]

To avoid letting the old man in, we must honestly answer this question: "Do I still believe the best is yet to come?" If not, we trend toward playing it safe—playing not to lose rather than playing to win.

That's why you need an internal converter to change the negative thought pattern into a productive one. When you think your best days are ahead of you, you know the greatest risk is not moving forward. Instead, you'll think, *What if my best days are still ahead?*

3. You Don't Really Know What You're Doing

I don't know why this thought pushed me around for so long before I converted it to something helpful. At some point, I realized this thought was true and it shouldn't bother me. *Of course I don't really know what I'm doing,* I reassured myself. *I've never done this before. I've never owned my own business. I've never launched out on my own. I'm a rookie. Very few rookies ever win the Most Valuable Player award in their first season.*

I chose to convert this thought from *I don't really know what I'm doing* to *I'm learning how to do something I've never done before.* This conversion changed how I was feeling. I saw myself as a learner, and learning requires failure.

To go back to what my friend David Butler says, "Don't ask, 'Is it working?' Ask, 'What am I learning?'" People who reinvent themselves make peace with the reality that they will learn as they go. In the early days of Buckhead Church, I asked the team to read *Building the Bridge as You Walk on It* by Robert Quinn.[39] The title alone described perfectly where we were.

While it's certainly helpful to find patterns to follow, what to do next will often require you to blaze your own path and create new patterns. This will inevitably lead to what seems like failure. It's actually learning in disguise.

4. This Situation Is Unique to You

This thought may not seem as stifling and problematic as the other three, but let me show you where it tripped me up. When I left Gwinnett Church in 2020 and entered the season of figuring out what was next, I began to see the challenges I encountered as ones no one had ever faced before. And while it's true, a global pandemic is usually a once-in-a-century kind of thing, people have faced all sorts of similar trials and tribulations.

The lessons are there if we look for them.

I went to San Francisco during my season of transition and had lunch with Brent Allen, who leads one of the most successful Chick-fil-A restaurants in the entire chain. Brent sponsored a business breakfast I spoke at near San Francisco. He was telling me that he grew up in Atlanta and that his dad had worked at Delta Air Lines, had done some work at Coca-Cola, and was now retired. As an Atlanta native, I love both of those organizations, and it's not unusual to meet people who have family members who worked at either location.

Joining us at lunch that day was our mutual friend Tyler Scott, the lead pastor of Community Presbyterian Church, where Brent attends. "Did Brent tell you who his dad is?" Tyler asked.

"Well, he said he worked at Delta and Coke," I replied.

Tyler smiled. "Brent's dad is Ron Allen, the former CEO of Delta and a Coca-Cola board member."

I looked at Brent and exclaimed, "Your dad is Ron Allen!" Again, as an Atlanta native, I knew, of course, of Ron Allen. He's an Atlanta legend.

If you read *Know What You're FOR*, you know I'm a big

believer in asking big. It didn't take me long to ask Brent if I could have lunch with his dad to learn and glean wisdom from him.

And it was at my first lunch with Ron Allen that I asked him questions about what he was pleased he had done as a leader; what his toughest lessons were; what sort of regrets, if any, he had; and what it was like to be on the Coke board.

Mr. Allen's answers reminded me that so many of life's challenges are the same. Sure, the company name may be different and the details may look nothing alike, but much of what we face is the same.

This helped me convert the thought of *This situation is unique to me* to *There's someone who has faced similar challenges, so seek them out.*

One of the best ways to convert negative thought patterns into productive ones is to put yourself around people who have "been there, done that." There's an old tried-and-true biblical principle that speaks to this: "As iron sharpens iron, so one person sharpens another."[40]

When you are pursuing what's next, you've got to be around sharpeners—people who are pursuing greater things in greater days. If not, your thoughts will get dull. You will be tempted to listen to fear, and the days of the past will look better than they really were.

Chances are if you're holding tightly to fear and believing your best days are behind you, it means you haven't listened to an iron sharpener lately. As uncomfortable as it is, the statement is true: we are the sum of the five people we spend the most time with in our lives.

Are you spending time with iron sharpeners? They are the best converters I know—those who know how to convert negative thought patterns into better thought patterns.

When the student is ready, the teacher will appear. It's how I found myself talking with another Atlanta legend and iron sharpener, the renowned politician and activist Ambassador Andrew Young. He never backed down from what's next, even though it meant facing situations he had never encountered. To illustrate, look at the new ground he took with each move:

- → pastor
- → civil rights leader
- → president of the Southern Christian Leadership Conference
- → congressman
- → United States ambassador to the United Nations
- → Two-time mayor of Atlanta
- → global businessman

→ partnered with Billy Payne to bring the Olympics to Atlanta

And that's a short list. One of the reasons I have been able to push through the fear of what's next is that I have tried to surround myself with people like Ambassador Young.

In *Know What You're FOR*, I shared the story of writing Ambassador Young a letter in which I asked if we could meet. Imagine my surprise when he said yes. This led to several opportunities to interview him for different events.

After I left Gwinnett Church, when I was feeling overwhelmed by all the change and the uncomfortable emotions that change always brings, I thought of Ambassador Young. I remember the story he tells of when he visited Dr.

I've had the opportunity to interview Ambassador Andrew Young on a few occasions, including this time at Buckhead Church.

Martin Luther King Jr. in that famous Birmingham jail and how he won over the prison guard through kindness. I also remember him telling me how lost he felt after Dr. King, not only someone he worked with but one of his best friends, was killed. I'll also remember him telling me how to deal with anger. "Don't get angry," he said. "Get smart."

I often remind myself that nothing I'm facing comes close to the challenges Ambassador Young had to overcome. Yet I know that the way he overcame obstacles provides patterns for me to follow.

That's the other thing the warm blanket of familiarity won't tell you. It won't tell you about the new people you'll meet through new pathways. It won't reveal the possibilities that await when you push off from shore. It won't tell you the space you can fill when you convert old ways of thinking into new, more productive ones.

All of which takes me back to my friend the turtle. Little did he know that as he was trying to climb to new heights and fell back, it would lead him to someone who was trying to climb new heights as well. All he needed was a little help from a new friend, which just happened to be me.

For today, maybe you need the same kind of help—a

lift to help you start converting those negative thought patterns into positive ones:

Thought Converters

What if this does work?

My best days are ahead of me.

I'm doing something I've never done before.

Someone has faced similar challenges; find an iron sharpener.

Keep climbing, keep striving, and continually convert those thoughts into new, positive patterns—and when you do, someone, somewhere, will come along to help you up, pick you up, and show you the way.

Just. Keep. Moving.

CHAPTER 11

It's Time

I remember calling Wendy and telling her, "I just got offered the dream job." We were a couple of years into launching Gwinnett Church, but my old life, the marketing one, came calling.

Other opportunities had arisen before, but none like this. This time, the money, the opportunity, and the people made us stop, catch our breath, and think. *Is this our next move?*

We did the pros and cons list. You know the one.

Pros

→ money
→ culture
→ opportunity
→ potential
→ people

The list kept growing on the pros side. The cons side was surprisingly short.

We turned it down anyway. Twice, in fact, after we were asked to reconsider.

This book has one simple aim and a hopeful goal: to help you know what to do next, or what not to do. These decisions come with risk, uncertainty, fear, gain, and loss. If we're not careful, though, we can let the unknown paralyze us by overanalyzing the decision—paralysis through analysis, as it's often called. We can analyze a decision away. At some point, we must decide.

A few years ago, I was able to tour Facebook's headquarters. I saw a large sign on the premises that read, "Done is better than perfect." That's a great perspective on what to do next. If you're looking for perfect, you'll probably stay on the sidelines.

No matter what you decide, you'll have days that cause you to wonder if you've made a mistake. It's all part of the journey. So I want to give you an overview of where we've come in order to help you know what's next:

→ You can't eliminate risk, but you can manage it.
→ Take the Career Risk Assessment.
→ Start where you are. Use what you have. Do what you can.

→ Pay attention to gifting, calling, and timing.

→ Build your network.

→ Create optimal options.

→ Develop a personal advisory board.

→ Climb the money wall.

→ The path to your dream job often leads through your day job.

→ Let go of past hurts, previous mistakes, and what others might say.

→ Convert negative thoughts into new positive patterns.

→ Just. Keep. Moving.

Before we close, I want to add one additional filter to think through: Don't build a life you won't enjoy.

Whatever comes next should serve us well. For example, when an opportunity comes up in this new season of running our own business, it's tempting to jump at each one and line them up one after another. After all, what if the opportunities stop coming?

> Don't build a life you won't enjoy.

But we don't want to work our life away. During our seasons of figuring out what's next, Wendy and I often said this out loud to one another: "Let's not build a life we won't enjoy."

We don't always get this right. Correction: I don't always get this right. Wendy does. She's great at reminding me that what comes next should be a step toward building a meaningful, worthwhile life. After all, you only get one shot at life. Sometimes this means saying no to good opportunities.

When we were considering this dream job offer, the list of pros far outnumbered the cons. And yet there was one con that outweighed them all in our opinion. Taking the dream job would negatively impact the time we would have with our family. I would need to get back on the road. I'd miss a lot of ball games and school events. And we're big believers in eating dinner together as a family. I'd miss those dinners as well. All of this weighed heavily on the con side.

It wasn't the last time Wendy and I would turn down an appealing offer. Over the years, we declined some incredible opportunities because we decided it wasn't the right time for our family.

It's hard to pass up good opportunities like this, especially when you don't see a long-term future where you currently are. That was our story. But our kids were thriving in their schools, and they loved the church. The season we were in was a season we would never get back. As hard as it was to turn down the dream job, that was a season where we needed to stay.

When you make a decision to stay, you're often tricked into buying a lie. There's a voice that whispers, *What if an opportunity like this never comes back around?* Sometimes it's an internal voice; other times it's an external one. "Are you crazy? This is the role of a lifetime!"

Being in your fifties has some benefits. Trust me, there are a lot of drawbacks too. (Like getting up in the morning and feeling like you sprained your ankle while you were asleep. How does that happen? I'll tell you. It's called your fifties.) One of the benefits, though, is that you have perspective.

You've seen good opportunities come and go, and you're aware of how good opportunities happen. Good opportunities flow to those who leverage their current opportunity. If you consistently bring your best, a better opportunity at the right time will eventually come around—the operative phrase being "the right time."

> Good opportunities flow to those who leverage their current opportunity.

And yes, decisions like these are personal ones. How Wendy and I decided to make our decisions isn't a filter you necessarily need to abide by or use. However, for us, we knew the season with our kids was a fleeting one, and we didn't want to miss it. What was next was doing what was best for our family. I passed up a lot of money because it came with a lot of travel. I had a lot of volleyball and soccer matches to attend. These were seasons literally within one large season of life. But looking back, it all seems so fast.

The other day, I was scrolling through photos on my phone and came across videos of Jesse serving in volleyball matches and Cole playing soccer. (By the way, text me and I'll send you the video of Cole scoring a goal as a goalie. And I'll show you one of the best left-handed volleyballers around!)

What was next for me in that season was being a present dad. Yes, I needed and wanted to be as effective as I could be in my career roles. I wanted to create optimal options for whatever the future might hold. But in that season, I wanted to choose my family. They were my best next step.

Maybe that's you right now. Maybe you've been offered the role of a lifetime. I get it. So was I. And I'll be honest, that particular role never came back around. It was a lot of money, a lot of prestige, and a lot of "corporate tax," as it's called. (A corporate tax refers to the tax you have to pay for the benefits of corporate life. And it's not exclusive to corporate life. There's a tax in all parts of life.)

Let me say it once more. This isn't a judgment zone.

You've got to make the decisions that are best for you and your family—whatever they may be. At some point, though, we all ultimately must answer the question, "What are we going to sacrifice?"

When our kids were younger, Wendy and I made a decision about parenting. We weren't going to consistently sacrifice time away from our kids, because we knew time would eventually take them away from us.

As Cole's senior year in high school progressed, we saw that time coming. As you know by now, my personal advisory board had given me the green light to start pursuing and dreaming of a life post-church and as a future empty nester. Not only that, we were paying attention to the momentum we were seeing with my book and the business breakfasts. We sensed that things were slowly changing, and we were being freed up to start taking some steps toward what was next.

One season was drawing to a close, and a new season was starting to open up. Looking back, I have no regrets about the money we walked away from and the opportunities we declined. You'll never regret choosing the most important people in your life.

A great question to ask as you consider what's next is, "How will this influence the people closest to me?" It's a hard question because it will come with a variety of answers, depending on who you ask. The simple fact that you asked and are willing to listen goes a long way. As my friend Daniel Harkavy reminds me, "Give your best to your best."

Choosing the most important people in your life over an opportunity is the right decision, but that doesn't make it any easier. In some ways, it's harder, especially if the money is enticing. Yet here I am—on the other side of it all. I'm profoundly grateful we sacrificed some things money can buy in order to experience the things it can't.

But again, please understand. I'm not laying a guilt trip on you if you made a different decision. It's not as much about what you did then as it is about what you can decide to do now.

If you have kids who are still at home and a decision is looming, involve them in the process. I've seen situations where parents drop a bomb on the kids. "Great news! Mom got a promotion, and we're moving to California!"—and the parents call me, perplexed because their kids are angry and hurt.

Imagine if someone were to drop a bomb like that on you. "Wait, what? You made this decision without me?" I'm not suggesting you let your kids make the decision. I am suggesting you involve them in the decision. There's a difference.

Situations like those are why, during my season of transition out of Gwinnett Church, Wendy and I found ourselves having lunch at Cheeky, our local Mexican restaurant, updating Jesse and Cole on our current thoughts about leaving. Jesse was home from college, and we wanted her to know the latest. We shared it was becoming more and more clear that our time was coming to an end and a new season was unfolding, but we wanted to hear what the kids thought.

What happened next may not seem like a big deal to you, but it's a moment I'll never forget. Jesse looked at me with tears in her eyes and said, "It's time, Dad. It's been a great season. We've loved it. But it's time."

I rarely get through telling that story without tears. In that moment, Wendy and I felt released—over chips and cheese dip, no less, which made it even better. There we were, having a serious life conversation with our grown-up kids, and it just made me so grateful.

I'm grateful for the seemingly uneventful family dinners, the bedtime stories when the kids were younger, and the events we attended through the years. I'm so grateful we said no to the right opportunities that came at the wrong time, knowing that eventually, somehow, someway, the right time would arrive.

The right opportunity at the right time isn't just the

right opportunity; it's a better one. And as I look back at lunch that day, it's as though I'm a few tables away, observing that moment. Amid the tears and cheese dip, Cole cracks a joke. We all laugh, and the conversation eventually turns to less serious matters . . . all the while, a chapter of our lives draws to a close and a new one unfolds.

What's next, as it always is, was on the way.

I'll Let You Decide

I remember what it was like on the day we left Gwinnett Church. Since then, it has felt like Wendy and I have lived five years in one. There have been twists and turns, ups and downs, wins and losses. We let go of what was in our hands in order to have something new placed in them. We grieved what we lost, while shifting our eyes toward what we gained. We let the fear wash over us, knowing it was like the tide that comes and goes, but the ocean of possibility is always there in the horizon. Through it all, we just kept walking.

The line from John Maxwell has been on repeat throughout this current season: "I never had a clear vision. I just kept moving forward."

That's my hope for you as we close. Just. Keep. Walking. Keep moving forward.

I'm not pleading with you to make a rash, unwise

decision. Neither do I want you to stay too long in a place where you begin to shrink down. Never shrink down to size to fit someone else's view of you. I've tried that. It's exhausting. Consistently shifting downward to a less-than-who-you-can-become version can fool you. On the surface it seems like it would be less taxing on you, but at the end of each day, your soul knows. You know.

You know there's more within you that needs to get out, to help the world become a better place. When your soul spins that knowledge over and over inside of you with no way out, it leads to an unhealthy sense of exhaustion.

I want something better for you. I want a healthy sense of exhaustion for you. Like a really great workout.

For example, one night I returned home from speaking in Houston, Texas. The event was with an amazing team from The Loken Group, and while I was very tired, it was a good tired. I had the opportunity to spend time with a great group of leaders I would have never met had I not ventured out and tapped into what else was within me.

I was exhausted but energized. That's a fun combination—and it's what I want for you. The world needs you to fill a larger space than what you think is possible. We need you to tap into a deeper well within you, which usually doesn't happen unless you step into what's next.

It's why you can't let the fear fool you. The circumstances may be different for everyone, but the hurdles are often the same. For example, I was talking to a friend who was really close to stepping into his next. Some financial risk was involved, as there usually is, so he was calling to give me an update and to ask for advice. He shared what another friend of ours had told him. "It's close enough. It's time to go. It's time to make the leap."

But he was still in a fight with uncertainty and fear. I get it. I've been there. It's why he was calling. "If you were to do this all over again, would you do it?" he asked me.

I told him about my experiences during a season of pursuing my next. I never thought I had what it takes to run my own business, until I had to. I never knew how challenging and rewarding starting a business would be for Wendy and me, until we found ourselves making decisions together. I never knew how hard it would be, and yet it wasn't as hard as I had feared.

"If you're going to pursue what's next, buckle up," I told him.

It's not going to be easy, but as you've heard me say before, that's not what we signed up for. Back to my friend's really good question though: "If you were to do this all over again, would you do it?"

I started our journey together in this book with a

picture. In fact, you may want to go back and take a look at it. If you look close enough, you may see the weariness, the fear, the doubt, the uncertainty—but you may also catch a glimpse of something else.

It's why I'm going to answer that question, "Would I do it all over again?" with another picture.

A couple of weeks before our one-year anniversary of stepping into what was next for us, Wendy and I were in California serving Community Presbyterian Church and the great work they're doing with FOR the Valley.

We found ourselves on the other side of the coun-try on a beautiful, somewhat chilly San Francisco morning—in a place we would never have been if we hadn't said yes to what was next. As Wendy and I sat at Fisherman's Wharf, sipping cups of coffee from Blue Bottle Coffee, which you can't get in the South, the contrast was a fitting analogy. We found ourselves in a place we had never been before. Would we do it all over again?

Well, I'll let you decide.

ACKNOWLEDGMENTS

I wrote this book while Wendy and I were living with her parents at their lake house. We had sold our house and were living in their basement before moving into our next home. The setting was fitting. We were in transition. Each morning, I woke up at 6:00 a.m. to write and watch the sunrise.

One of my favorite authors, Mark Batterson, advises writers to think of the reader while they write. If you're reading this, in a very real sense, I was thinking of you during those 6:00 a.m. writing sessions at the lake. Thanks for the inspiration and company.

One of the best (and necessary) parts of a healthy next is a great group of friends you can trust. Wendy and I have been blessed with an amazing support group.

For example, my friends at Maxwell Leadership believed in me in a time when I needed it. I'm forever grateful for John Maxwell, Mark Cole, Chad Johnson, Kimberly Whetsell, Lane Jones, Norwood Davis, Chris Goede, Chris Robinson, Jason Brooks, Linda Eggers, Becky Bursell, John Griffin, Matt Reardon, Michelle Oostenburg, Robert

Sindon, George Hopkins, Jake Decker, Jason Stoughton, Lorna Weston-Smyth, Taylor Melton, and the entire team. You lead well because . . . everyone deserves to be led well.

To the wonderful team at The FOR Company—Wendy Henderson, Lauren Espy, Alyssa Kang, Jacqui Uhler, and Belinda Randall—thank you for working with me during such a pivotal season. I'm forever grateful, and I'll see you at Ted's.

To my Chick-fil-A family, thank you for your friendship over two decades now. You are an important part of our story. Thanks to these friends who were an extra-pivotal part of our first year of next: Andrew Cathy, Shane Benson, David Farmer, Tim Tassopoulos, Reade Tidwell, Susannah Frost, Cliff Robinson, Dana Latasa, Jon Bridges, Mark Miller, Teneya Fouts, Rita Blanding, Priscilla Nicholson, Keith Lyons, and many more.

This was my second time working with the team at Zondervan, and it was even better this time around. Thank you, Andy Rogers, for your belief and fantastic help and insights, as well as for cheering on the Braves during their World Series win in 2021. Thanks as well to Webster Younce, Dirk Buursma, and the rest of the Zondervan family for your continued support in both *Know What You're FOR* and now *What to Do Next*. I'm looking forward to our third book next year.

It was during a conversation with Zondervan and Maxwell Leadership that my agent Matt Yates suggested the word *next* to describe the content I was writing. Instantly, I knew that was the word. Thanks, Matt. And another shout-out to Alyssa Kang, who designed the cover in one of her many moments of brilliance at our FOR Company office.

I'm grateful to my in-laws, Peggy and Everett Major, for letting me borrow those 6:00 a.m. sunrises on the lake to write this. Wendy is my muse, my inspiration, followed next by Jesse and Cole. This book is dedicated to both of you because I know God has great plans and next chapters awaiting you. And to my wonderful mom—here's hoping your Hawks win an NBA championship and you meet Trae Young in the process.

Finally, thank you to you, the reader. Here's my cell number: (404) 317-3946. After reading this, please text me with your takeaways and how I can help. Before we close, I offer one final word of encouragement. While staying with friends Mallory and David Farmer, I noticed a framed art piece outside my room. It was a quote from Esther 4:14, and I knew it was no accident that I saw this. I knew I was supposed to pass this word of encouragement to each of you as you pursue what's next. As you finish this book, turn back to the opening pages, read again the words adapted from Esther 4:14, and remember the potential and promise of what's next. It won't be easy, but you didn't sign up for easy; you signed up for worthwhile.

NOTES

1. Cited in Ian Cook, "Who Is Driving the Great Resignation?," *Harvard Business Review*, September 15, 2021, https://hbr.org/2021/09/who-is-driving-the-great-resignation; see also Britney Nguyen, "Here's Everything We Know about 'The Great Resignation,' Who's Quitting, and Why," *MSN Money*, September 22, 2021, www.msn.com/en-us/money/careersandeducation/heres-everything-we-know-about-the-great-resignation-whos-quitting-and-why/ar-AAOHRxB.
2. A. L. Patterson, "Shamgar: Start Where You Are, Use What You Have, Do What You Can," posted by Kevin Williams, January 5, 2017, YouTube video, 1:01:49, www.youtube.com/watch?v=BUg704JKIe0.
3. Max De Pree, *Leadership Is an Art* (New York: Currency, 2004), 11.
4. "Should I Stay or Should I Go," track 3 on The Clash, *Combat Rock*, CBS Records, 1982.
5. John C. Maxwell, *Leadershift: The 11 Essential Changes Every Leader Must Embrace* (New York: HarperCollins Leadership, 2019), 14.
6. Donald Miller, *Business Made Simple: 60 Days to Master Leadership, Sales, Marketing, Execution, Management,*

Personal Productivity and More (New York: HarperCollins Leadership, 2021), 26.

7. See John Maxwell, *The 21 Irrefutable Laws of Leadership: Follow Them and People Will Follow You,* rev. ed. (New York: HarperCollins Leadership, 2007), 1–10.

8. T. D. Jakes (@ BishopJakes), Twitter post, February 16, 2018, 11:59 a.m., https://twitter.com/bishopjakes/status/964544891094257665.

9. Quoted in Andrew Hill with John Wooden, *Be Quick—But Don't Hurry!* (New York: Simon & Schuster, 2001), 69.

10. Proverbs 13:12.

11. See Gardiner Morse, "The Science behind Six Degrees," *Harvard Business Review,* February 2003, https://hbr.org/2003/02/the-science-behind-six-degrees.

12. John Maxwell, *Good Leaders Ask Great Questions: Your Foundation for Successful Leadership* (New York: Center Street, 2014), 24.

13. Og Mandino, *The Greatest Salesman in the World* (1968; repr., New York: Bantam, 1985), 93.

14. "Right Now," track 9 on Van Halen, *For Unlawful Carnal Knowledge,* Warner Bros. Records, 1991.

15. For more on a personal board, see Jim Collins, "Looking Out for Number One," *Inc.,* June 1996, www.jimcollins.com/article_topics/articles/looking-out.html.

16. Proverbs 15:22.

17. See Stephen R. Covey, *The 7 Habits of Highly Effective People: Restoring the Character Ethic* (1989; repr., New York: Simon & Schuster, 2013), 159–64.

18. Chuck Allen, *Cool Change* podcast, https://podcasts .apple.com/us/podcast/cool-change/id1517675668?i =1000512600985.

19. Carey Nieuwhof, "Marathon (2): Grieve Your Losses," *Carey Nieuwhof* (blog), March 2010, https://careynieuwhof .com/grieve-losses.

20. See Brian Rashid, "20 Speakers You Shouldn't Miss the Opportunity to See," *Forbes*, June 17, 2017, www.forbes .com/sites/brianrashid/2017/06/17/20-speakers-you -shouldnt-miss-the-opportunity-to-see.

21. Marcus Buckingham and Donald O. Clifton, *Now, Discover Your Strengths* (New York: Free Press, 2001).

22. "Working for the Weekend," track 1 on Loverboy, *Get Lucky*, Columbia Records, 1981.

23. *Rocky III*, directed by Sylvester Stallone, starring Sylvester Stallone, Carl Weathers, and Mr. T (Beverly Hills, CA: MGM/UA Entertainment Co., 1982), DVD.

24. *Rocky III*.

25. Dr. Henry Cloud, *Necessary Endings* (New York: HarperCollins, 2010), 7.

26. Lewis B. Smedes, *Forgive and Forget: Healing the Hurts We Don't Deserve* (1984; repr., San Francisco: HarperOne, 1996), 133.

27. Bruce Wilkinson, *The Freedom Factor: Finding Peace by Forgiving Others . . . and Yourself* (Portland, OR: Zeal Books, 2016).

28. Lysa TerKeurst, *Forgiving What You Can't Forget* (Nashville: Nelson, 2020), 29, 104.

29. Quoted in Bob Jones, "Four Ways to Bounce Back after a Loss," ABNWT, January 14, 2021, https://abnwt.com /articles/four-ways-to-bounce-back-after-a-loss.

30. Quoted in Mike Berardino, "Mike Tyson Explains One of His Most Famous Quotes," *Sun Sentinel* (Fort Lauderdale, FL), November 9, 2012, www.sun-sentinel.com/sfl-mike -tyson-explains-one-of-his-most-famous-quotes-20121109 -story.html.

31. Guy Raz, "Live Episode! Jeni's Splendid Ice Creams: Jeni Britton Bauer," February 28, 2018, in *How I Built This*, produced by NPR, podcast, MP3 audio, www.npr.org /2018/02/28/589158213/live-episode-jenis-splendid-ice -creams-jeni-britton-bauer.

32. See Hiten Shah, "How Slack Became a $16 Billion Business by Making Work Less Boring," *Nira* (blog), https://nira.com/slack-history.

33. Miller, *Business Made Simple*, 9–12.

34. Ryan Holiday, *The Obstacle Is the Way: The Timeless Art of Turning Trials into Triumph* (New York: Portfolio/ Penguin, 2014).

35. "Mama Said," track 1 on The Shirelles, *The Shirelles Sing to Trumpets and Strings*, Scepter Records, 1961.

36. *The Dark Knight Rises*, directed by Christopher Nolan, starring Christian Bale and Tom Hardy, (Burbank, CA: Warner Bros. Pictures, 2012), DVD.

37. Randy Ross and David Salyers, *Remarkable! Maximizing Results through Value Creation* (Grand Rapids: Baker, 2016).

38. Quoted in Tom Blake, "On Life and Love after 50: 'Don't Let the Old Man In,'" *SC Times*, June 11, 2020, www.sanclementetimes.com/on-life-and-love-after-50 -dont-let-the-old-man-in.

39. Robert E. Quinn, *Building the Bridge as You Walk on It: A Guide for Leading Change* (San Francisco: Jossey-Bass, 2004).

40. Proverbs 27:17.

Know What You're FOR

A Growth Strategy for Work,
An Even Better Strategy for Life

Jeff Henderson

Your organization—business, church, or nonprofit—will experience unprecedented growth when you close the gap between these two game-changing questions: What are we known for? What do we want to be known for?

In *Know What You're FOR*, entrepreneur and thought leader Jeff Henderson makes it clear that if we want to change the world with our products or our mission, we must shift the focus of our messaging and marketing. Rather than self-promoting, we must transform our organizations to be people-centric. Whether you're a business leader, a change advocate, or a movement maker, *Know What You're FOR* will help you—and your organization—thrive.

Working with companies like Chick-fil-A and the Atlanta Braves, then serving as a pastor for fifteen years at North Point Ministries, Jeff knows what success looks like for healthy organizations and healthy lives. He equips you with a simple strategy and tools for extraordinary growth. You'll discover how to:

- work FOR your current and future customers with a new, effective method;
- be FOR your team and help your people reach full potential;
- create a ripple impact by being FOR your community; and
- live and work your best by caring FOR yourself.

In a hypercritical, cynical world, let's be a group of people known for who and what we're FOR. It's a powerful strategy for business. But more importantly, it is a revolutionary way to live.

Available in stores and online!